Richard F.S. Tarr

Indus Valley Painted Pottery

Richard F.S. Tarr

Indus Valley Painted Pottery

ISBN/EAN: 9783337385484

Printed in Europe, USA, Canada, Australia, Japan

Cover: Foto ©Thomas Meinert / pixelio.de

More available books at **www.hansebooks.com**

INDUS VALLEY
PAINTED POTTERY

A Comparative Study
of the Designs on the Painted Wares
of the Harappa Culture

BY RICHARD F. S. STARR

PRINCETON
PRINCETON UNIVERSITY PRESS
LONDON: HUMPHREY MILFORD, OXFORD UNIVERSITY PRESS
1941

THIS PUBLICATION OF THIS VOLUME HAS BEEN AIDED BY GRANTS
FROM THE AMERICAN COUNCIL OF LEARNED SOCIETIES
AND THE INSTITUTE FOR ADVANCED STUDY

FOREWORD

THIS volume is not, nor could it be, so complete and conclusive a discussion of the subject as to pretend solution to all its riddles and answers to all its questions. The mysteries of prehistoric interrelationships could not be so easily or fully penetrated. It is, rather, the hope of the author that this work will help to clarify and stimulate future and further discussions in this field; and if the data and suggestions in the following pages help to an appreciable degree in clearing away the haze that has surrounded the Indus Valley in its relationship to other portions of the ancient world, the real purpose of this work will have been accomplished.

This study originated in 1938 as a dissertation presented to Princeton University in candidacy for the degree of Doctor of Philosophy. Since then, it has been entirely revised and rewritten; the less important material has been eliminated and much has been added that was originally overlooked or has been newly discovered.

So many people have given their assistance in this work that it is difficult to acknowledge my gratitude to each individually. However, I wish first of all to mention the assistance given by my wife. Not only her uncomplaining and interminable labor at typing, retyping and proofreading, but her clear-sighted criticism has been of enormous help. Among those in the academic world I am especially indebted to Professor Harold H. Bender and Professor Philip K. Hitti for their continual and willing assistance, both of a scholarly and material nature, and I wish here to emphasize my obligation to them. Professor Ernst Herzfeld, with his usual generosity, has given me much of his time and, as always, his comments have been stimulating, penetrating and wise. I wish also to thank Professor W. Norman Brown and Dr. Ananda Coomaraswamy for reading my manuscript and for offering many helpful suggestions. Nor should I neglect to record my indebtedness to the Institute for Advanced Study which made it possible for me to carry on the revision of my original manuscript. Finally, it is a distinct pleasure to express my gratitude to the American Council of Learned Societies and to the Institute for Advanced Study for making possible the publication of this volume.

R. F. S. STARR

Princeton, February 1941.

TABLE OF CONTENTS

[vii]

FIGURES IN THE TEXT

The site at which each illustrated specimen was found is given first, then the publication in which the figure originally appeared. Where the name of the site and the abbreviation used to denote the publication correspond, only the publication reference is given.

[xiii]

ABBREVIATIONS

A.J.A.	*American Journal of Archaeology.*
al-'Ubaid	H. R. Hall and C. Leonard Woolley, *Al-'Ubaid* (Oxford, 1927).
A.R.A.S.I.	*Annual Report of the Archaeological Survey of India.*
Arpachiyah	M. E. L. Mallowan and R. Cruikshank Rose, *The Excavations at Tall Arpachiyah, 1933* (Oxford, 1935; reprinted in book form from *Iraq*, vol. II, pt. I).
Bull. A.I.I.A.A.	*Bulletin, American Institute for Iranian Art and Archaeology.*
Bull. A.S.O.R.	*Bulletin, American Schools of Oriental Research.*
Bull. M.F.A.	Ernest Mackay, "Excavations at Chanhu-daro by the American School of Indic and Iranian Studies and the Museum of Fine Arts, Boston: Season 1935-36," *Bulletin, Museum of Fine Arts, Boston*, vol. XXXIV, no. 205 (Oct., 1936).
Chagar Bazar	M. E. L. Mallowan, "The Excavations at Tall Chagar Bazar and an Archaeological Survey of the Ḥabur Region, 1934-5," *Iraq*, vol. III, pt. I (Spring, 1936).
Del. en Perse	*Mémoires de la Délégation en Perse* (Paris).
Gedrosia	Sir Aurel Stein, *An Archaeological Tour in Gedrosia*, Memoir no. 43 (Calcutta, 1931).
Giyan	G. Contenau and R. Ghirshman, *Fouilles du Tépé Giyan* (Paris, 1935).
Gawra	E. A. Speiser, *Excavations at Tepe Gawra* (Philadelphia, 1935).
Halaf	Dr. Baron Max von Oppenheim, *Tell Halaf*, tr. Gerald Wheeler (New York, n.d.).
Hissar	Erich F. Schmidt, *Excavations at Tepe Hissar, Damghan* (Philadelphia, 1937).
Ill. Lond. News	*Illustrated London News.*
Inn. Asia	Sir Aurel Stein, *Innermost Asia* (Oxford, 1928).
Jemdet Nasr	Ernest Mackay, "Report on Excavations at Jemdet Nasr, Iraq," *Field Museum, Anthropology, Memoirs*, vol. I, no. 3 (Chicago, 1931).
Liv. Annals	*Annals of Archaeology and Anthropology*, University of Liverpool.
M-d	*Mohenjo-daro and the Indus Civilization*, ed. Sir John Marshall (London, 1931), vols. I-III.

[2]

M-d. 1927-31   E. J. H. Mackay, *Further Excavations at Mohenjo-daro*
                    (Delhi, 1938), vols. I-II.
Memoir   Memoir of the Indian Archaeological Survey.
Nal   H. Hargreaves, *Excavations in Baluchistan 1925, Sam-
                    pur Mound, Mushang and Sohr Damb, Nal*, Memoir
                    no. 35 (Calcutta, 1929).
Nineveh, 1931-32   R. Campbell Thompson and M. E. L. Mallowan, "The
                    British Museum Excavations at Nineveh, 1931-32,"
                    Liv. Annals, vol. XX, no. 1-4 (Nov., 1933).
Niphauanda   Ernst Herzfeld, *Niphauanda*, Iranische Denkmäler,
                    lief. 3/4 (Berlin, 1933).
North Baluchistan   Sir Aurel Stein, *An Archaeological Tour in Waziristan
                    and Northern Baluchistan*, Memoir no. 37 (Calcutta,
                    1929).
Nuzi   Richard F. S. Starr, *Nuzi*, vol. II (Harvard University
                    Press, 1937).
O.I.C.   *Oriental Institute Communications*, University of Chi-
                    cago.
Persepolis   Ernst Herzfeld, *Steinzeitlicher Hügel bei Persepolis*,
                    Iranische Denkmäler, lief. 1 & 2 (Berlin, 1932).
Persian Art   *A Survey of Persian Art*, ed. Arthur Upham Pope
                    (Oxford University Press, 1938).
Persis   Sir Aurel Stein, "An Archaeological Tour in the An-
                    cient Persis," *Iraq*, vol. III, pt. 2 (Autumn, 1936).
Reconn.   Sir Aurel Stein, *Archaeological Reconnaissances in
                    North-western India and South-eastern Irān* (London,
                    1937).
Samarra   Ernst Herzfeld, *Die vorgeschichtlichen Töpfereien von
                    Samarra. Die Ausgrabungen von Samarra, V* (Berlin,
                    1930).
Shah Tepe   T. J. Arne, "Swedish Archaeological Expedition to
                    Iran 1932-1933," *Acta Archaeologica*, vol. VI, fasc. 1-2
                    (1935).
Sialk   R. Ghirshman, *Fouilles de Sialk, près de Kashan, 1933,
                    1934, 1937* (Paris, 1938), vol. I.
Sind   N. G. Majumdar, *Explorations in Sind*, Memoir no. 48
                    (Delhi, 1934).
Studies   H. Frankfort, *Studies in Early Pottery of the Near
                    East*, vol. I (London, 1924).
Turkestan   Raphael Pumpelly, *Explorations in Turkestan, Expedi-
                    tion of 1904* (Washington, 1908), vol. I.

PART I

INTRODUCTION

I

SCHOLARS interested in those remote periods when Oriental man
was struggling toward the edge of history had for long concen-
trated their attention either on the Near East or on distant China.
Prehistoric India, it seemed, had nothing to offer comparable in
antiquity and material development. Yet within the last two
decades the situation has changed. Intensive archaeological inves-
tigations at ancient sites along the Indus River in northwestern
India have laid bare the remnants of a civilization far greater in
antiquity than anything previously known as Indian.

The first of these excavations was started in 1920 in the mound
Harappa,[1] in the Punjab, and the importance of the finds led to
the commencement of the great excavations at Mohenjo-daro in
Sind in 1921.[2] The results revealed a non-Aryan civilization, clearly

[1] Isolated surface finds from Harappa, of a type that later was to be recognized as
"Indus Valley prehistoric," were known as early as the winter of 1872-73; see Alexander
Cunningham, *Archaeological Survey of India: Report for the Year 1872-73* (Calcutta,
1875), pp. 105-8. Note: the location of all the ancient sites mentioned in the text will
be found on the map at the back.

[2] See *M-d* for the first detailed discussion of the buildings and objects of Mohenjo-
daro and selected objects from Harappa. For preliminary reports on the excavations at

[5]

prehistoric so far as India is concerned, and in some ways far in advance of Sumer and Elam, its nearest comparable neighbors. The scientific world which had long considered Sumer as the peer of early Asiatic cultures suddenly found itself confronted by another claimant from this entirely unexpected quarter. Nowhere in antiquity had so high a degree of civic prosperity been reached at such an early date, and nowhere in the Ancient East was there a people who seem to have been less baited by princes, priests and war. The amazing absence of what may properly be called palaces and temples, and the scarcity of weapons of offense, attest this. Nowhere in antiquity has life appeared so ordered and secure. And if we lack the spiritual concepts found elsewhere, or the wealth of works of art, it should be remembered, first, that the vast majority of their writings has quite certainly perished and that what little is left to us is still undecipherable, and second, that archaeological research among these people is still in its infancy.

However, imposing as this early Indus civilization is in its architectural monuments, and accomplished though it may be in city planning, metal working, and sculpture, it is its painted pottery that presents the closest likeness to other, better known, early cultures in Asia. One finds it repeatedly stated that analogies exist between the painted pottery of Mohenjo-daro and that of other Iranian, Elamitic or Mesopotamian prehistoric peoples. It is the purpose here to compare critically the designs on this Indian ware with those found to the west. In doing this we will discover what justification there is for these assertions of likeness. More important still, through such a study we can determine the status of this ware (and to a certain extent the whole culture which produced it) in relation to the great painted pottery family of Western Asia.

II

In dealing here only with the painted pottery designs, certain normally significant factors in pottery study will of necessity be relegated to a position of second importance. The pigments used,

Mohenjo-daro, Harappa. and other Indus Valley sites, see *A.R.A.S.I.*, 1930-31. 1923-23 through 1935-36. The latest detailed discussion of Mohenjo-daro is found in *M-d.* 1927-31.

[6]

and the color and treatment of the background, for example, are factors of lesser constancy and must concern us less than the designs themselves. One need hardly point out the numerous examples in Mesopotamia and Iran of the persistence of early elements of painted pottery design into successively later periods, each differing as to pigments and background. Also clearly less stable are the composition of the clay body of the vessels and the quality of the firing. With these factors we are also hampered by their general unreliability when concerned with relatively small groups of specimens undistinguished by constant peculiarities, such as is the case with the Indus Valley material, and the lack of fully detailed information on composition and condition both in the case of India and many of our western wares. The shapes of the vessels help us much less than one might hope. This is due largely to the rarity of complete Indus Valley painted specimens, or of sherds sufficiently large to give a reliable indication of the original outline. However, we may assume that the Indian painted ware did not differ markedly in shape from the unpainted, since the few complete painted specimens agree perfectly with the unpainted.

One difficulty, that of nomenclature, should be settled first. A variety of names has been used in designating the prehistoric Indian pottery and culture first unearthed at Harappa and best exemplified by the finds of Mohenjo-daro. Most common is "Indus Valley," yet this is obviously unsatisfactory, for the Indus Valley has in recent years produced concrete evidence of at least five distinct cultures, each clearly prehistoric. Consequently, I propose to follow the lead of Ernest Mackay* in the use of the term "Harappa" as a generic name, after the precedent set in the Nearer East of naming a ware or culture after its point of first discovery. The other prehistoric Indian wares will be similarly treated in this discussion.

It is not the purpose here to assign precise dates to the known phases of Harappan culture, nor to any of the other cultures or sites with which comparisons will be made. However, the sequence in which the Mesopotamian prehistoric cultures appear, and their

* *Bull. M.F.A.*, p. 83.

[7]

general relation to each other, is well known. The sequence relationship of the Iranian and Elamitic cultures to each other, and to those of Mesopotamia, is less clear, but certain tentative conclusions as to their interrelationship may be drawn. Since all will be used for comparison in the discussion that is to follow, they are shown in the appended table in the relationship which, in the light of present evidence, seems substantially correct. It is obvious, of course, that objections can be made to these proposed sequences of Iranian and Elamitic groups, but this is not particularly pertinent to our study as a whole, nor does it affect in any way our individual

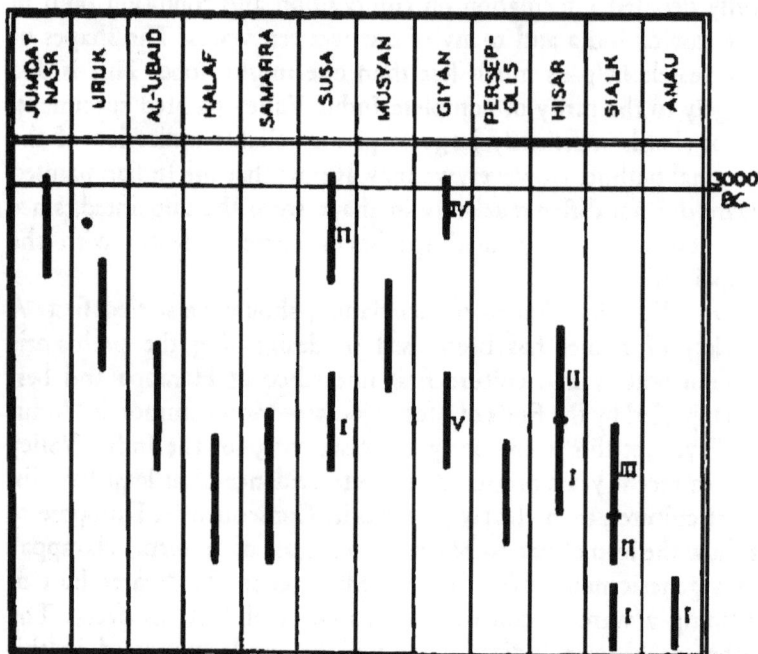

JUMDAT NASR	URUK	AL-'UBAID	HALAF	SAMARRA	SUSA	MUSYAN	GIYAN	PERSEP-OLIS	HISAR	SIALK	ANAU

comparisons with Harappan examples. No attempt has been made to include the scores of sites somewhat hastily trenched by Sir Aurel Stein during his reconnaissances north and west of the Indus; many have recognizable relationships east and west, as will be pointed out later. It should be remembered that the following table

[8]

is a purely schematic representation. It does not attempt to fix the duration of time in years for any one people, but only the relation of their known period of existence to that of other prehistoric peoples.

III

Harappa ware is compared here only with that from the north and west. One would expect at least traces of some relationship with the south, for there is a certain amount of indicative though inconclusive evidence that the Harappans were in some way related to the Dravidians, associated in our minds today primarily with the south of India,[4] and we will point out later certain non-western, presumably Indian characteristics in the painted pottery designs; yet so far not so much as a single surface sherd even remotely comparable to Harappa ware has been reported from southern or eastern India, in spite of the fact that two decades have now elapsed since the importance of this ware was first recognized. Furthermore, painted pottery of the character presented by Harappa, Iran, and Mesopotamia is distinctly a northern phenomenon. Nowhere in Asia is a similar technique found south of the twenty-fifth parallel, except at the mouth of the Indus itself and at an "Indus culture" outpost on the Kathiawar Peninsula.[5] It would be strange indeed for it not to have been already reported had it been a truly southern as well as a northern means of expression.

One peculiar difficulty connected with a comparison between the pottery of Harappa and the prehistoric pottery of Iran and Mesopotamia is the clear disparity in time between the two. No exact date limits for the Harappan culture can yet be fixed, but we do have such a striking body of parallels to dated Sumer that it is possible to say with certainty that the Harappan civilization as we see it at Mohenjo-daro, Harappa, and Chanhu-daro flour-

---

[4] Possible Harappa-Dravida relationships are necessarily outside the scope of this work, but a thorough study, and particularly further field work in the south, is essential before we can hope for an unbiased picture of the position of the Harappans in prehistoric India as a whole. For the pointers toward such a relationship see Marshall in *M-d*, chaps. v, viii. For opposing evidence, based on a linguistic study, see A. S. C. Ross, *The "Numeral-Signs" of the Mohenjo-Daro Script*, Memoir, no. 57 (Delhi, 1938).

[5] See p. 14.

ished during the third millennium before Christ, at least from the time of the Royal Tombs of Ur through the Third Dynasty of Ur (approximately 2850-2300 B.C.). Earlier than that we have only the presence of certain Harappan conventions on the Jumdat Nasr period seals of Elam,[*] and the assurance that so developed a state of civilization as we first see it at Harappa and Mohenjo-daro must have had a history going far beyond the earliest limit just mentioned. We find, on looking at Mesopotamia, that our latest comparable painted pottery, Jumdat Nasr, is, at its latest, scarcely younger than 3000 B.C., and that prior to Jumdat Nasr came Uruk, al-'Ubaid, Tell Halaf and Samarra.[*] In Elam we find Susa I far more ancient than 2850 B.C., and only Susa II overlapping with the terminus definitely established for Harappa. In Iran we find a similar condition, Persepolis, Sialk, and Tepe Hisar I being far anterior to our known Harappa, while only the upper levels of Tepe Hisar, Tepe Giyan and related sites produced painted ware within the period in which Harappan remains have actually been found.

In the light of these conditions, we could not hope for any particularly close parallels in composition as a whole between the Harappan and the older Iranian and Mesopotamian painted designs even if we assume that the younger were the direct descendants of the older ones. However, it is of interest that similarities in the decorative elements making up the more complex Harappan designs can be detected, and that they relate more often to the earlier than to the later foreign wares.

Both Sir John Marshall and Ernest Mackay, who was in charge of the greater part of the Mohenjo-daro field work, comment on the remarkably static nature of the material finds

[*] See pp. 83-4.

[*] In the rendering of geographical names used throughout the following text the accepted Anglicization has intentionally been used, wherever it does not stray too far from the correct transliteration. For example, one will find "Halaf" or "Persiano-ghundai," used without vocalic or other diacritical marks, rather than the strictly correct forms Ḥalāf and Persiano-ghundai. However, occasional corrections to the accepted forms have been introduced: for example, "Jumdat Nasr" for the more common Jemdet Nasr or Jamdat Nasr, and "Hisar" (strictly speaking, Hisâr in place of the usual rendering Hissar. The more precise transliteration is to be found here only in the list of sites at the end of the volume, under the heading Map.

at Harappan sites. In the pottery, for example, there is but little✓ change in character between the earliest and the latest of the superimposed levels thus far uncovered at Mohenjo-daro, though there is a diminution in the quantity of painted ware in the later strata. This lack of change is a point of importance, for it indicates that pottery decoration was a tradition long fixed and faithfully retained, thus carrying our Harappan products back close in time to the prehistoric Iranian and Mesopotamian wares. Coupled with this lack of change, the diminution in the quantity of painted ware suggests that the practice of painting was one retained only for special, perhaps ritualistic, purposes into a time when the more common output of the kiln had discarded such archaisms.

IV

The question will arise as to how justified one may be in considering that every decorative unit, every principle of technique must be an inheritance from earlier times and peoples. Certainly these must be discovered for the first time quite alone by some given set of people. Why, then, should they not be discovered again quite independently by other peoples? There is nothing particularly advanced, it would seem, in the use of triangles, wavy line, or parallel straight lines as the basis for a geometrical composition. That might occur to any people independently. But the question is not quite as simple as that, for we cannot always look upon these single decorative elements as simple geometrical figures, conceived as such and used without meaning. They cannot always be considered as the basic elements from which a more complicated geometrical design may be built up, but rather, they are often the irreducible minimum by which a more complicated and naturalistic design may be expressed. We have from Susa I, for example, rows of birds with long vertical necks used as a border on the lips of vessels. No one would mistake them for anything else, but when the design is more simplified, as it often is, it is only a slight protuberance or jut at the top or bottom that shows these parallel lines to represent rows of birds and not mere space-filling by a geometrically-minded potter.

When, from the same site, we find the lines similarly placed, but without even the slight distinguishing marks seen in the intermediate stages, we have some reason for believing that they still represent birds though the means has changed from pictographic to symbolic. In the same manner, a wavy line may represent a river; sweeping curved lines, or even circles, a mountain goat with its big horns; triangles, the bodies of animals, and so on, though the meaning of the symbol is not usually clear unless one has seen it in some of its intermediate stages. It must also be clear from this that much which we consider as merely meaningless ornament on prehistoric ware represents, in reality, specific objects or concepts, the nature of which we cannot interpret as yet.

It is uncertain whether or not these symbols are necessarily the result of a long evolutionary period. In the earlier cultures—Susa I for example—we find pictorial representation and the symbol for the same or related objects used side by side, sometimes even on the same vessel.[*] Evidently to the primitive potter it was immaterial whether a given idea was represented one way or the other, since both produced the same image in the mind and each was individually capable of producing an aesthetically satisfying design. Even the usual belief that the picture came first is open to some question. Be that as it may, we must assume a period of development extending far beyond the earliest painted designs we now have. No other assumption is possible when we consider the highly developed, even sophisticated, artistic sense of the earliest decorators, and the amazing spread in prehistoric times of certain identical artistic conventions over the whole of north-central Asia.

Certain pitfalls that one may encounter in analyzing prehistoric pottery designs have just been mentioned. One should beware, however, of giving to every geometrical unit an inner meaning which actually it may not have had by the time the design was drawn. It is perfectly true that under certain conditions a wavy line, let us say, between rows of opposed triangles represented a stream flowing between mountains, but that cannot

[*] Cf. Del. en Perse, xiii, pl. xlii, 5, bird symbols.

mean that forever after wavy line and triangle held only this meaning, even in the hands of the direct descendants of the original pictorial decorators. Somewhere in the line of inheritors, artists were bound to come who used these elements because of their usefulness in achieving a definite composition and not because they wished to represent specific phenomena. It may even have been forgotten that certain decorative elements once stood for these phenomena. It is hard, for example, to see in most of the geometrical designs of al-'Ubaid and in many of the patterns of Tell Halaf ware any vestiges of pictorial art. We should also consider the possibility that among certain peoples painted designs originated purely as geometrical decoration and not as pictorial representation. This cannot be proven, but one is reminded of the possibility by the total lack of naturalism in such very primitive pottery as Anau I.

The task of distinguishing between these decorative elements on painted pottery which are symbols for some more complex scene or object and those which have lost, or never had, a symbolic value is difficult in all but the most obvious examples. For the most part we must content ourselves with pointing out such few symbolic values as may be deemed certain, remembering that others may also be present, though unrecognizable or unacceptable in the light of our present knowledge.

V

The great excavations at Mohenjo-daro, as published by Sir John Marshall and Dr. Mackay, are the source of most of our knowledge of Harappan materials as a whole. Besides this, we have the finds from Chanhu-daro and Harappa itself, partially published in various journals.[9] Second in importance only to the Mohenjo-daro volumes is the account of explorations carried out in Sind by N. G. Majumdar.[10] From this, more than from any other source, we see the spread of Harappan culture up and down the Indus. Unfortunately, his work was confined to Sind,

[9] For Mohenjo-daro and Harappa, see p. 5, n. 2, supra. For Chanhu-daro, see Bull. M.F.A.; Ill. Lond. News, Nov. 14 and 21; 1936: A.R.A.S.I., 1935-36.
[10] Explorations in Sind, Memoir no. 48 (Delhi, 1934).

[13]

and until we have a similar survey of the Punjab we can only assume that a like concentration extended at least as far as Harappa itself. How far southeast and northwest the Harappans extended we cannot tell at present. Nothing unmistakably Harappan has been found farther southeast of the Indus than the valley itself. However, directly south of the lower Indus, on the neck of the Kathiawar Peninsula, an outpost of what at least may be called "Indus culture" has been reported. Here at a site called Rangpur, twenty miles southeast of Limbdi, trial trenches have exposed a quantity of painted shreds which have been equated with the Late Period pottery of Mohenjo-daro.[11] There is some doubt as to whether these finds may be considered as true representatives of Harappan culture—the designs, at least, show closer affinities to those of the Amri culture than to Harappa—but they certainly can be considered as a coastal, southern extention of the general Indus Valley painted pottery technique beyond the confines of the valley itself. On the northwest, unmistakable Harappan ware has been found more than a hundred and fifty miles from the river.[12] How great was the total extent of these peoples during the third millennium one cannot tell. Yet their present known habitat, an expanse at least six hundred miles long and two hundred miles wide, compares favorably with even the most widespread of other Asiatic prehistoric cultures. The relative homogeneity of the Harappan material over this whole area and the aspect of permanence in its known cities gives the impression of a unified people, long and firmly established in the land.

As to the pottery, the body of the vessels shows no noticeable difference in composition between the plain and the painted wares. Almost all are wheel-made; and all but the smallest show the use of a degraissant, usually sand or lime, to temper the raw clay. The clay was certainly local and came from the kiln pink or light red in color.[13] All the Harappan pottery, whether plain or painted, is heavy sturdy ware, in marked contrast to the

[11] A.R.A.S.I., 1934-35, pp. 34-8.
[12] Zik and Mehi, Cedrosia, pl. xxi, Zik. 5; pl. xxx, Mehi. II. 4. 5.
[13] With the exception of the dark gray ware which is outside our study. See M-d, pl. lxxxiii, 28-43.

delicate thinness of much of the Iranian and Mesopotamian prehistoric fabrics.)

If one were to interpret the term "painted pottery" literally, it
would demand the inclusion of a large group of Harappan vessels
which, though painted, are almost useless for comparative purposes.
This group consists of many vessels, unornamented except for
horizontal bands of one or more simple painted lines. The decoration here has the appearance of complete degeneration. Nothing
seems to remain of the older tradition of decoration except a
hurried compliance to an ancient custom, performed in the easiest
possible manner. In effect it has ceased to be "painted pottery," for
the term as usually applied implies an effort on the part of the
primitive artist to depict, in so far as he is able, an aesthetically
satisfying scene, whether it be straight pictorial, symbolic, or
merely a pleasing pattern. But here the lines have actually become
a structural accompaniment to the vessels so decorated, emphasiz-
ing a given member, such as neck, shoulder, or lip, or imitating
the incised horizontal lines for which they are so often an obvious
substitute. Nevertheless, this decadent form of expression has its
value, as will be pointed out later, in helping to explain the static
and somewhat uninspired character of much that may more gen-
uinely be called the "painted ware" of Harappan sites.

The physical difference between the ware that is ornamented
merely with simple horizontal bands and that which we choose,
somewhat arbitrarily, to call Harappan "painted pottery" lies in
the preparation of the surface to be painted. The simple bands
on the first group are painted directly on the body of the vessel,
while the decoration of the second is always applied on a wash
or slip covering the body. Slips, far more common than washes,
are relatively poor in adhesion and scale off easily on exposure
after excavation. The colors used are cream, buff, pink, and light
or dark red, the first three being natural clay colors and the last
two (the most common) the result of an addition of red ochre.[14]
Most of the surfaces so produced, and particularly the red, were
polished to give a fine lustrous effect, the long vertical strokes of

[14] No mention is made in any of the publications as to the exact thickness of the slip.
M-d (p. 320) says of the red, "This slip is invariably thick. . . ."

[15]

the burnisher being perceptible on the specimens of better pre-
servation. Vessels are frequently slipped only on that portion
destined for painted decoration, rather than over the whole of
the exterior, and rare examples of the use of slips of two different
colors on different parts of the same vessel have been reported.[18]
It is on the smooth surface so created that the painted design
was applied. Black, in the form of manganiferous hematite, is the
usual pigment of the painted designs, and varies in intensity from
brown to a rich purple-black. Red, the color so common in the
painted wares to the west, is rarely used by itself, but appears
usually as a background for designs painted in black. White and
yellow had some popularity as ground colors, and a few examples
of an unstable powdery green have been reported. The red, the
black, and even the white are before-baking pigments, the green
apparently being applied after baking. Though the painting in the
majority of cases is monochromatic, the effect is one of bichromy
since the background through its brilliance and warmth of tone
has a chromatic rather than a neutral value. In the same way, the
examples of polychromy are intensified by the color value of the
background. The decoration was disposed in horizontal registers
extending downward as far as, and sometimes beyond, the center
of the vessel. The more naturalistic elements of design appear in
these registers framed by simple banded or geometrical borders. A
few bowls exist painted over their whole exterior.[19] Interior
decoration is exceedingly rare.

VI

In a comparison between the painted designs of Harappa and
those of the west, one would normally turn to the wares of Baluchistan—the first stage westward from the Indus—for here there
is a considerable body of pottery, interrelated as to pottery design
both within Baluchistan and with the Indus, yet divisible into
several distinct pottery groups. Unfortunately, this helps us less
than had been hoped. Comparing it with Harappa we are confronted not with a dearth of parallels but with an overabundance

18 M-d, p. 320; M-d, 1927-31, pp. 178-9.   19 See fig. 33, infra.

of similar points. This is of value in that it shows a close interrelationship between the various Baluchistan wares and Harappa, yet there are but few indications by which one may establish their chronological relationship. It is true that undeniable Harappan motifs occur among the finds from many of the Baluchistan sites, proving that the Baluchi ware is contemporaneous with some phase of Harappan existence; but we cannot tell at what point in the history of our one well-stratified Harappan site—Mohenjo-daro —these finds fall. It is certain that Harappan culture—and its painted pottery—existed before the time of the earliest levels yet exposed at Mohenjo-daro, and there is no reason for believing that it ceased with the desertion of Mohenjo-daro as a cosmopolitan center. Thus any one, or all, of the Baluchi cultures may have flourished either before, or contemporaneously with, or after the period of Harappa as it has been exposed so far at Mohenjo-daro.

None of the Baluchi pottery designs has about it the "feel" of antiquity such as can be safely attributed to Susa I, Halaf, or Persepolis in the west. Nor is there any conclusive archaeological evidence by which their relationship in time to each other may be judged. But the fact that the pottery is consistently made on the fast wheel, as well as the constant association of these finds with copper and their frequent similarity to and association with Harappan decorative motifs, would suggest that they come late in the prehistoric period.)

With the distinctive ware first found at Nal in Baluchistan there are some pointers toward a relative date. At Shahi-tump in western British Makran, Sir Aurel Stein exposed habitation levels the finds of which he equated in style, roughly, with such sites as Kulli and Mehi further east.[17] Undeniable likeness of design exists, but in the light of more recent work in Iran the ware of these Shahi-tump habitation levels seems more closely related to the earlier Persian fabrics. Nevertheless, the similarity between the Shahi-tump copper stamp seals and others of clay from the late Iranian culture level of Tepe Hisar III, and a triple bowl—of the type known from Susa II and from the late gray-ware cultures of Iran as seen at Shah Tepe—assure it a relatively late date in the prehistory of

[17] Gedrosia, passim.

the East as a whole.[18] Overlying and separated from these strata were graves with pottery betraying certain characteristics peculiar to Nal ware. Consequently, Stein is justified in considering Nal a late prehistoric development. Ernest Mackay, on the other hand, considers it as early. The pottery, he says, ". . . more or less approximates to the pottery of the first period of Susa," which assigns it, in a cautious way, to a very early period.[19] The reason for this opinion is the prevalence of the step pattern at both Nal and Susa I, as well as the use of other decorative elements found at both sites. It is perfectly true that there is a certain likeness and that certain patterns or elements are common to both, but we will see that the same is true between Susa I and Harappa, though we know that Harappa in its known levels cannot "approximate" to the period of Susa I. Marshall, too, considers it "earlier than any yet exposed at Mohenjo-daro or Harappa," basing his opinion on the likeness to certain Susa I motifs.[20] It would seem that both Mackay and Marshall are postulating a relationship in time on tenuous evidence. There can be no doubt that Nal and Susa I are in some way related, but when we see how the early decorative elements persist throughout the history of painted pottery in Asia, it would be unsafe to consider their presence the sole proof of contemporaneity.

Even without Stein's evidence, Nal must be considered as late; certainly not earlier than Harappa and probably later than the early and middle strata at Mohenjo-daro. In the first place, if we consider Nal as earlier, we must also believe that the designs which Nal and Harappa have in common were in a sense inherited by Harappa from Nal. Yet in the Nal examples we have a certain heavy sureness of line that is quite different both from the painstaking delicacy of the best Harappan examples and the bold irregularities of the majority.[21] Besides that, in the Nal animal drawings there is an anatomical exactness and realism unlike

[18] *Ibid.*, pl. xiv, Sh. T. ii. 20, etc.; *Hissar*, pl. xlix, H 257ß, etc.; *Gedrosia*, pl. xiii, Sh. T. vi. 3; *Del. en Perse*, xiii, pl. xxxii, 9; *Shah Tepe*, fig. 29. See also the triple bowl of the Jhangar period from Chanhu-daro, *Ill. Lond. News*, Nov. 21, 1936, p. 910.
[19] *M-d*, p. 322.   [20] *M-d*, p. 100, n. 3.
[21] Cf. *Nal*, pl. xxi, 1-4 and *infra*. figs. 131 and 155.

anything in Harappa and infinitely more sophisticated than the highly conventionalized animal forms of Susa I and earlier wares. Compare, for example, the lithe figure of the lion of *Nal*, pl. xxi, 8, or the ease with which the ibex with turned head is shown in *Nal*, pl. xxi, 14, with anything from Harappa or from early Elam. There can be no question that we have to deal here with a technique infinitely more advanced than Susa I. The fact that Harappan designs are found at Nal sites does not demand that Nal be even contemporary with the Harappan culture exposed at Mohenjo-daro. The peculiarly static nature of Harappan designs implies that they would continue to persist long after Mohenjo-daro had ceased to exist as a city.

However, the purpose of this study is not the establishment of dates for the Baluchistan wares. This cannot be done with any exactitude, and even a comparative chronology relating in its proper order one site to another is hazardous in most cases until we have more than the results of trial trenches on which to go. Nor is it intended to analyze the style of the multitudinous specimens of painted ware from Baluchistan. Sir John Marshall's study of these wares should remain our guide, for it is based on a first-hand knowledge of the sherds themselves.[22] His analysis seems beyond question, though there will be occasion later to question some of his conclusions. Suffice it to say that the groups into which he has divided the Baluchi wares represent a refinement in classification with which we need not bother here. It is a listing of the species within a genus, for no one can look at this material as a whole without seeing that it all received its fundamental character from one source. In making his comparisons and in drawing attention to the subtle distinctions that mark one of his proposed subdivisions from another, he has naturally been forced to dwell extensively on their differences. But if one considers, instead, their likenesses, they appear in a quite different light. One can see in the ware of Kulli, Mehi, and Periano-ghundai, to mention but a few, a resemblance so close to the Harappan in its decorative elements that we must consider them as collateral and closely related

[22] *M-d*, pp. 96-101. For a geographically more comprehensive summary see V. G. Childe, *New Light on the Most Ancient East* (London, 1934), pp. 269-83.

branches of the same basic culture in so far as the painted designs alone are taken as our evidence. Because of this obvious interrelationship, various Baluchi specimens of painted design will be presented in the following discussion, not as substitutes for Harappan examples, or as their equivalent, but as representatives of the broad eastern family of which Harappa is a member.

VII

With the various fabrics of the Indus Valley itself we are confronted with fewer difficulties, for their relationship in time to each other is quite clearly understood. The pottery of four distinct prehistoric cultures, other than Harappa, has been found in the Indus Valley: Amri, Jhukar, Jhangar, and an as yet unnamed pottery from a cemetery overlying Harappa itself.[23] That of Jhukar follows Harappa in period, and Jhangar (unpainted incised gray ware) in turn succeeds Jhukar. There is less certainty of the relationship of the "Harappa cemetery" ware to Jhukar and Jhangar, but it is demonstrably later than Harappa; judging from its radical differences in style, it is certainly alien to Jhukar and Jhangar culturally, and it is in all probability considerably later in date. Since Jhukar, Jhangar, and "Harappa cemetery" are all younger than Harappa proper, they will figure but little in our study which of necessity must deal largely with sites demonstrably older than the Harappan levels now exposed. It should be added, however, that in painted pottery motifs, Jhukar shows as close a relationship to Harappa as the most similar of the Baluchi wares. There can be no question that the cultural relationship between the two—Harappa and Jhukar—is very close indeed, though it would seem that they were collateral branches of the same family rather than ancestor and inheritor.

[23] Amri, Jhukar and Jhangar, so far as is known, are found only in Sind, "Harappa cemetery" only in the Punjab. For Amri see *Sind*; for Jhukar, *Sind, Bull. M.F.A.*, and *Ill. Lond. News*, Nov. 14 and 21, 1936; for Jhangar, *Bull. M.F.A.*; for "Harappa cemetery," *A.R.A.S.I.*, 1930-34, pt. I, pp. 72-90. Variants have been found differing so markedly from the basic pottery styles of the above cultures that they may eventually come to be considered as still other distinct Indus Valley cultures. See particularly such sites as Lal Chhatto and Mashak in *Sind*, pp. 60-3; pl. xxiii.

Amri ware, the final non-Harappan fabric of the Indus Valley to be noted, presents a somewhat different situation. This distinctive pottery was first discovered at the ancient site known today as Amri, situated on the banks of the Indus some eighty miles south of Mohenjo-daro. So far, fifteen sites have been discovered—all in Sind—in which pottery of Amri type is the distinguishing feature.[14] Little of a distinctive nature, other than the pottery, has been unearthed from the Amri levels of these sites, but the flint and chert blades common to both Harappa and to the chalcolithic and copper-age sites of all western Asia are liberally represented.

The important feature of the Amri finds is that in several instances they occur in the same mounds in which Harappa ware is found, and that in every case where the site is sufficiently intact to permit a close study of the stratification—Amri, Lohri, Ghazi Shah and Pandi Wahi—the Amri ware underlay that of Harappa. At the last two of the four sites just mentioned there is a certain ✓ amount of intermingling of Amri and Harappa wares where the two strata meet, showing that though Amri is the earlier, there was a brief period in which both existed at the same sites simultaneously. Moreover, we have among the Amri objects, copper and vitreous paste bangles showing that the finds fall within the same general age as Harappa. At the same time, the fact that Amri and Harappa sherds appear for a brief interval side by side, each distinct from the other, shows that Harappa is not an outgrowth of Amri, but a distinct cultural entity in itself.

Majumdar has quite correctly pointed out the close similarity of Amri pottery to the South Baluchistan wares of Kulli, Mehi, and kindred sites, as well as to that of Periano-ghundai and Moghul-ghundai farther north in Baluchistan.[20] There is no question that the two—Amri and the Baluchistan wares here noted—were the products of the same broad cultural group.

[14] See the following sites described in Sind: Tharro, p. 20; Lohri, p. 65; Ghazi Shah, p. 79; Tando Rahim Khan. p. 86; Gorandi, p. 87; Pandi Wahi, p. 91; Damb Buthi, p. 114; Baadhai, p. 120; Dhal, p. 126; Pokhran, p. 128; Kohtras Buthi, p. 132; Khajur Landi, p. 134; Arabjo Thana, p. 136; Othmanjo Buthi, p. 140; Dhillanijo-kot, p. 145.

[20] Sind, p. 27-8.

[21]

To state the Amri characteristics briefly: the ware is moderately thin and is wheel-thrown; the surface is covered, usually, with a thin slip or wash of the same color as the body of the pot, which, depending on the condition of the firing, turns to a buff, cream or pink color. On this the design is painted in black and reddish-brown—polychromy—after the vessel has been fired.

Let us compare definite Amri and Harappa designs. The ubiquitous horizontal bands, looped lines and lozenges, of course, are present in both, as well as the ever-present wavy lines and triangles. Compare, though, the like treatment of the triangles in the Amri specimen seen in Fig. 53 (*infra*) and Harappa Fig. 54, or the sigma pattern of Amri Fig. 56 and Harappa Fig. 55. The use of blocks of vertical lines between horizontals is the same in Amri and Harappa, and we have in both subdivisions the checkerboard pattern. In Amri Fig. 12 and Harappa Fig. 11 we have basically the same motif of vertical lines suspended from loops. Nor is there any difference basically between the idea represented in Amri Fig. 90 and that in Harappa Fig. 89. In Amri we have hooked lines springing from a perpendicular identical with that of Harappa Fig. 165, and almost complete identity between the horn motif of Amri Fig. 164 and Harappa Fig. 163. Both use the ancient comb motif: Amri Fig. 83 and Harappa Fig. 79.

The principal difference between the designs of Amri and those of Harappa lies in the Harappan preference for floral rather than geometrical motifs alone. It should be noted that the difference here is not one of execution but of quantity. The relative thinness of the Amri ware compared with most Harappan ware is the greatest point of mechanical contrast between the two, though the later date of Harappa and the wholesale method of manufacture that intensively urban life would imply, might serve as an explanation. The difference in the tone of the background is the one on which Sir John Marshall places the greatest emphasis in his classification of Indian and Baluchi wares. Yet it will be shown later that whether or not a pottery group shows predominantly a light or a dark ground is purely a matter of local or group preference and not a sure guide to fundamental differences of origination. Moreover, it should be remembered that Harappan ware is not uniformly dark in background; only the majority is so treated. The difference of polychromy is also relative, Amri using it only more consistently than Harappa. The after-baking pigments represent a difference only in the degree of use, for Harappa used them quite certainly in the evanescent green pigment.

The pottery of Amri has been dealt with here at some length because as the direct predecessor of Harappa in the Indus Valley, and because of the close relationship between the decorative elements in the painted pottery designs of the two, it will be called upon in our comparison between Harappa and the west more frequently than any other of the Indus or Baluchistan fabrics.

PART II

HARAPPAN RELATIONSHIPS WITH IRAN
AND MESOPOTAMIA

LET us now take up in details the individual decorative units
that make up Harappan painted designs, seeing, if possible, what
significant similarities they may have in common with the painted
wares of the west. We will treat first those units that are wholly
geometrical in appearance as well as those whose natuŗalistic
origin is perceptible even though they have become conventionalized to the point where the image from which they sprang
is no longer obvious. The patently naturalistic patterns will follow
later.

I

Straight-line borders. Beginning with the simplest of patterns,
the single line (or multiple continuous lines) which separates
vases into registers or panels, we have the most common motif in
the painted pottery world. Fig. 1 shows it in its simplest though
probably not its most elemental form, and throughout the illustrations to follow it will be seen repeated over and over again as a
border for more complex patterns (Fig. 36, etc.). Though usually
horizontal, it appears at Harappa, and elsewhere, also as a vertical
border separating individual panels of design (Fig. 151). It is
probable that such decoration was not the first to be conceived, but
it certainly must have been among the first improvements once
the primitive artist began to give serious consideration to the
aesthetic possibilities of design. It serves not only to separate scenes

[25]

and panels, but also as a frame, giving accent, directness, and order to the more decorative elements within. Nowhere in the painted pottery areas of the East is this lacking, though the very ancient painted pottery of Anau I, from Turkestan, uses it the least.

Straight lines used in combination become the foundations of the infinitely more complex patterns to be considered later. However, there is one grouping sufficiently elemental to justify inclusion at this point. This is the simple pattern formed by connecting long horizontal lines with closely grouped verticals or diagonals. The use of verticals as a space filler is an extremely common convention in the early wares of Iran and Mesopotamia. As a divider between metopes we have the Harappan example, Fig. 67. The

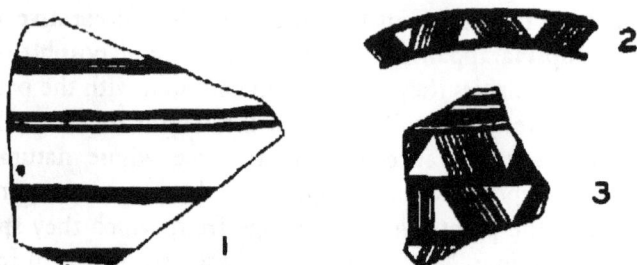

same treatment is found in the west as early as Halaf, and became a favorite method of separation at Musyan. Closely spaced diagonal lines, in one form or another, are found almost universally throughout western fabrics, but among the earlier wares we have from Samarra[1] an example close in spirit to our Harappan example, Fig. 2. It is not until we reach the relatively modern wares of Susa II and Nehavand[2] that we find an abundant use of verticals and diagonals truly similar to our Harappan examples, Figs. 2 and 3.

II

Loop patterns. The ubiquitous looped line appears in Harappan designs (Figs. 4, 121, 140, 156) though it is not common. It usually lacks the regularity or the emphasis seen in the earlier wares and

[1] *Samarra*, pl. xiix, 45.
[2] Susa II: *Del. en Perse.* xiii, pl. xxxi, etc. Nehavand: *Niphamanda*, pl. iii, 3.

thus loses its true decorative value. In most of its Harappan appear-
ances it has degenerated into a stylistic convention employed with
little true sense of its usefulness as an effective decorative motif.

There are a number of cases, however, where this motif is used
with full effectiveness, though it no longer is seen in its simplest
form. In Fig. 5, at the top, we have what is essentially a loop
pattern. Here it is raised above the line rather than suspended
from it, and the enclosed spaces are filled with crosshatching.
Again, in the border of the Amri specimen, Fig. 42, we see it in
the same position with somewhat the same impression of solidity
seen in Fig. 5, due to the heaviness of its outline. There is plenty of
precedent for the raised rather than the suspended loop; it was

commonly used in the al-'Ubaid and Tell Halaf pottery[3] and it is
a natural result where a wavy line touches a lower horizontal one.

What seems to be an interesting Harappan variation of the loop
pattern is seen in Fig. 6 in which the loop ceases to be a portion
of a continuous line and stands free. There is no clear precedent
for independent loops used in horizontal rows, but the value of the
bold, free loop was known and most effectively used not only by
the potters of the al-'Ubaid period but also by those of the Khurab
in Iran.[4] In Fig. 173 we see another example in which the background forms the design of the loop. This should be compared
with an identical border from Ja'farabad in the environs of Susa,[5]
found in association with sherds similar in style to those of Musyan,

[3] *Arpachiyah*, fig. 30, 4; fig. 78, 17.
[4] Al-'Ubaid: *Arpachiyah*, fig. 32, 1-2; fig. 35, 1, 6. Khurab: *Reconn.*, pl. xvii, B. ii. 204.
[5] *Del. en Perse*, xx, fig. 20, 8.

west of Susa. The practice seen here, of painting the background so that the unpainted portion forms the design, is found throughout the Persepolis pottery,[4] and the same principle is used on the stone stamp seals of Tepe Hisar I.

What would appear to be the inevitable development of the continuous loop pattern is seen in the Mohenjo-daro specimen, Fig. 7, commonly known as the fish-scale pattern. That this is a logical outgrowth of the continuous loop seems certain from the manner in which two or three bands of loops are similarly treated in the pottery of the Tell Halaf period.[5] That potters of this same early period also used it as an all-over design is seen in other examples from the Tell Halaf period.[6] It is interesting that this design does not appear in the pottery of Samarra, Susa I, al-'Ubaid, Musyan, or Jundat Nasr; in other words, it does not seem to have been discovered by any of the prehistoric potters of Elam and southern Mesopotamia.[7] In Iran it is well developed in Sialk III,

and at Tepe Giyan, in Level V (the earliest), there is an experimentation with four rows of attached loops[10] similar to those just cited for the Halaf levels of Arpachiyah. But no examples are found in our earlier Iranian culture levels, such as Sialk I and II, and Persepolis. However, several examples are known from Tal-i-skau, in Fars, which is culturally close to Persepolis.[11] From

[4] *Persepolis*, pl. xv, 2, etc.   [5] *Arpachiyah*, fig. 64, 4; fig. 70, 3.
[6] *Ibid.*, fig. 7B, 19, 20.
[7] It does appear, however, in the prehistoric levels at Nuzi which, though not in the south, correspond to al-'Ubaid. See *Nuzi*, pl. 47, Q.
[10] *Giyan*, pl. 53.   [11] *Persis*, pl. xxiv, 29, 30, 38.

Tal-i-regi (Khusu) in Fars, we have the specimen shown in Fig. 8 in association with sherds having the appearance of a developed Persepolis style. This should be compared with the Harappan example, Fig. 9. In both examples the scales are decorated, one by vertical lines (at Tal-i-skau by horizontal and diagonal lines, and by W's), the other by dots. This avoidance of empty spaces is a common phenomenon among undeveloped artists and is particularly impelling in Harappan pottery. Another Harappan example, Fig. 10, shows this same desire to fill the empty spaces within the scales, but in this case the artist had the intersecting-circle pattern in mind in using the crow's-foot design that is here the filler.

It is significant that the loop pattern was not in favor in the most primitive Oriental fabrics. Instead, we have rows of contiguous triangles—either solid or open—used in the same manner in which later one would find the loop pattern. This suggests that the continuous loop is an outgrowth of this more primitive, angular form. In the proto-Halaf wares of Mersin, for example, the loop does not appear, but instead, there are triangle borders, composed either of solid figures or of evenly zigzagging lines.[11] In Anau I bands of triangles were in particular favor, and in certain instances one can see what may well be the origin of the loop motif in the rounding of the outlines of these normally angular patterns.[12] In Sialk I the loop is definitely established, though the triangle band is more common; moreover, the two patterns—loop and triangle border—were used there interchangeably, suggesting that the loop was but a more cursive form of the triangle border.

Our most interesting variant of the loop pattern is that illustrated by the Harappan example, Fig. 11, and the Amri specimen, Fig. 12. Here the continuous loop has vertical lines added to it, extending sometimes as far as the lower border. This is an extremely ancient pattern and one of widespread popularity. It appears frequently as a border in the Samarra pottery, always in the manner illustrated in Fig. 13.[13] In the Tell Halaf period it is again

[11] *Liv. Annals*, xxvi, pl. xxix, 2, 7, 9.   [12] *Turkestan*, pl. 28, 2; etc.
[13] See also the identical specimen from Nineveh 2 in *Nineveh 1931-32*, pl. xxxviii, 3.

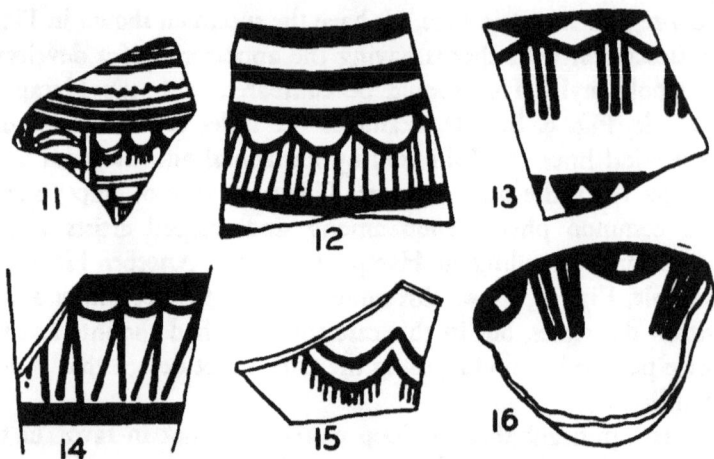

common, though here the pendant lines are usually double rather than triple (Fig. 14). One minor difference from the Indian examples will be noted in the position of the pendants, in that they drop from the *junction* of the loops rather than from the belly of the loop as in Fig. 11, or from all parts of it as in Fig. 12. This need not bother us, for we have from the Halaf levels of Chagar Bazar[15] examples corresponding quite closely to Fig. 12, and in Fig. 15, which illustrates a sherd from Kalat-i-gird in extreme eastern Kirman, in the Helmand Delta, we have an almost exact parallel to Fig. 11.[16]

Between the geographical extremes of Tell Halaf and Kirman we have a number of other occurrences of this motif. Most ancient of all is one from Sialk I—a specimen but little different in its essentials from the Samarra example illustrated in Fig. 13.[17] From Tal-i-skau in Fars we have the specimen illustrated in Fig. 16. The finds from this site, as pointed out above, are closely related to those

[15] *Chagar Bazar*, pl. ii, 4.

[16] See also *Inn. Ana*, pl. cxiii, Md. (R.R.) II. 013, from Ram-rud (from the same region and illustrated on the same plate is also our fig. 15). Considerable difficulty confronts one in assigning the prehistoric pottery from the Helmand Delta to any given culture or period, for millenia of intense wind-erosion have cut away the ancient habitation levels and left the heavier objects, early and late alike, exposed together on the surface. Many of the designs, however, bear a distinct likeness to those of Persepolis.

[17] *Sialk*, pl. xxxix, S. 1426.

of Persepolis, and it should be noted that again there is no fundamental difference between this example and Fig. 13 from
Samarra. A variant, related both to Figs. 16 and 11, is found
at Tal-i-Sang-i-siah in Fars among sherds of a developed Persepolis
style.[18] From the earliest levels of Tepe Giyan (Level V) we have
another variant of the Samarra-Persepolis version and still another
one resembling the Indian example, Fig. 12.[19] Finally, in level
IB of Tepe Hisar, we have a further set of parallels with the Indian
example, Fig. 12. Fig. 17 from Hisar seems to show the design

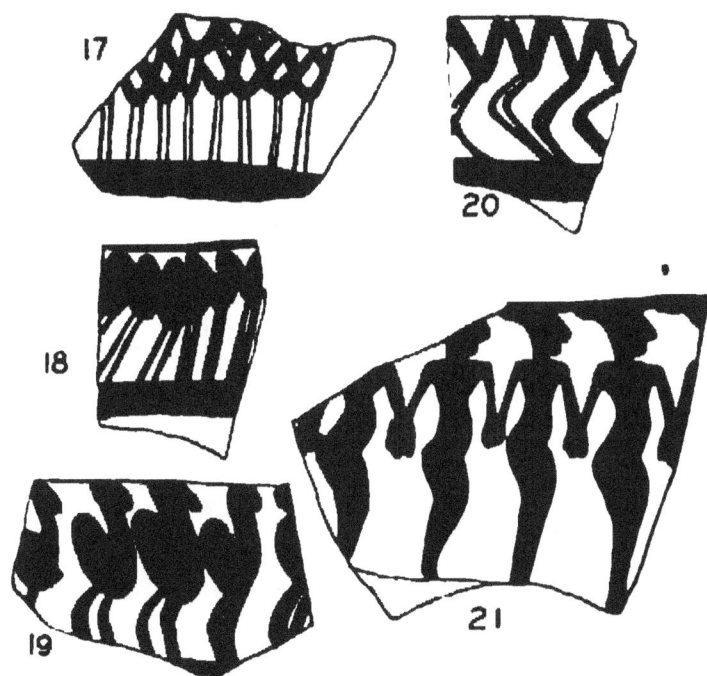

in a degenerated form, if one may judge from the carelessness of
the workmanship; nor is Fig. 18 appreciably better, though it goes
back to the loop and pendant concept more closely than Fig. 17.
There is no way of telling whether the loops in Fig. 17 are the
lowest row of an extended fish-scale pattern or whether it was

[18] *Perui.* pl. xxiii, 65.   [19] *Giy in.* pl. 40, 53.

merely an inadept rendering of the double row of loops seen in Fig. 13 from Samarra.

We have, in respect to the Hisar examples, an interesting sidelight on this pattern. The connection between Fig. 19 and Fig. 18, or at least the reasonable probability of a connection, is quite clear. The only fundamental difference between these two Hisar designs is that in Fig. 19 the loop is broken and that at the end of each section so created is added a projection to make the separate units into birds. Consequently, one wonders whether or not in Tepe Hisar the loop with pendant lines is a degeneration of a row of birds or people. Fig. 20 from Hisar, for example, might well be a slightly more realistic conventionalization (than Fig. 18) of the row of birds seen in Fig. 19. Or one might say that in Fig. 20 we have a stylization of people linked together in a dance, just as people dance in the Orient today, and that related to it is the scene depicted on the contemporary sherd from Cheshmeh 'Ali near Teheran, shown in Fig. 21, and the row of humans on a sherd from Khazineh.[20]

Considering the possibility that here we have a stylization of humans, Fig. 14 from the Halaf levels of Arpachiyah could easily be interpreted as a line of people linked together. Continuing on this idea, it is of interest to look at Fig. 22 from Tell Halaf itself.

Here there would seem no doubt that humans are being represented and in this case the more or less vertical strokes would simply serve to indicate the skirt. The question will then arise as to why, if this whole motif is a stylization of humans, do most of the patterns show three or more pendant lines rather than two. In all probability the lines merely serve as a simplification of the skirted lower body which in Fig. 22 is shown in more graphic

[20] *Del. en Perse*, VIII, fig. 254. See also the figures from Sialk III: *Sialk*, pls. lxxv, lxxx, C, 6-8.

fashion. A case in point is another sherd from Tell Halaf, illustrated in Fig. 23. Von Oppenheim considers these figures to be humans,[11] and I think he is correct. There is little doubt that we have here a line of figures shoulder to shoulder just as the figures in Figs. 14 and 22 stand side by side, hand linked to hand. If this be the case, the pendant lines below what appear as short tunics—or perhaps just the convenient geometric rendering of the trunk—would be an abbreviation of the skirt lines of Fig. 22. This seems a reasonable assumption, particularly when one considers the unambiguous way in which legs as such are shown in Figs. 14, 17-20, and 25.

If we accept this interpretation of the Halaf-period members of this motif, we can well understand how the design such as that seen at Samarra (Fig. 13) can have become the symbol for man.[12] One may wonder whether it retained that symbolism throughout the years and across the space separating Tell Halaf from India, along the course in which we have just traced it, for the specimen from Fars, Fig. 16, was certainly early enough to have been within the time when such a symbolic meaning would have been understood; yet here it has come to be treated as a decorative motif without strict adherence to the principle of the essential two or three pendant members used to denote humans.[13] However, the symbolic value was at least partially understood as late as the time of Hisar IB as can be seen by its merger at that time with the animal forms illustrated in Figs. 18 and 19.

Evidence for the survival of the knowledge of this proposed symbolic value into Harappan times is found at Rana-ghundai in Baluchistan in the design illustrated in Fig. 24.[14] The similarity to the form of Fig. 14 is clear, while the extention of the linked

- [11] *Halaf*, caption under pl. liii. Cf. also *Arpachiyah*, fig. 77, 19 for an almost identical specimen of Samarra-type ware, on which there are groups of both two and three pendant lines. Seen also at Sakje-Geuzi, west of Tell Halaf: *Lir. Annals*, xxiv, pl. xxv, 1; and *Chagar Bazar*, fig. 37, 23.

[12] This interpretation has already been advanced by Mallowan in *Chagar Bazar*, p. 49.

[13] Equally early is a figure from Sialk II, which may also be a symbol for man; in Sialk III there is a design remarkably similar in its essentials to that of fig. 23: *Sialk*, pls. xlviii, C, 10; lxix, S. 67.

[14] The original illustration in which this sherd appears is somewhat unclear, but there is an indication that the "legs" of the figure on the left actually consist of three strokes as do those of the center figure.

[33]

24   25

"hands" downward seems but an exaggeration of the arrangement noted in Fig. 22. The most striking feature, however, is the flowing lines at the "head." This distinctly calls to mind the Samarra figure with flowing locks (Fig. 25), which is unquestionably human in form. This twofold similarity in our Baluchi specimen, to the Halaf symbol on one hand and the Samarra picture on the other, would leave little doubt that the symbol did represent man, and that we have it here, in this relatively late period, sufficiently understood as such to be treated both symbolically and pictorially. Fig. 24, incidentally, may be the connecting link between the curious hair form of the Samarra figures and the very similar hair treatment in the much later figures depicted on the "Harappa cemetery" ware.[25]

If we are correct in considering the loop with pendant lines as a symbol for man, we have several examples in which symbolic and pictorial representations are used for the same subject in the same level of one culture, as mentioned in the Introduction. To cite but one case, compare the stylized and conventionalized forms of Figs. 14, 22, and 23 with the labored attempts at depicting humans pictorially seen in *Halaf,* pl. li, 8 or pl. liii, 11, 12, and 18. Quite obviously the primitive artist was more adept in depicting the abstraction, though he had no scruples in using either as the mood or conditions demanded.[26]

III

Wavy line (river pattern). There would at first appearance seem to be little difference between the elemental band of con-

[25] *A.R.A.S.I.,* 1930-34, pt. ii, pl. xxvii, b.
[26] For a recent, differing proposal as to the origin both of the simple loop and the loop with pendants see *Bull. A.I.I.A.A.,* v, pp. 63-9.

tinuous loops and the usual wavy line seen so often on prehistoric
pottery throughout Asia. The wavy line used as a border on the
Harappan example, Fig. 26, for instance, might have been a variation of the loop pattern which for aesthetic reasons was given a
more flowing, less abrupt line, rather than a representation of an

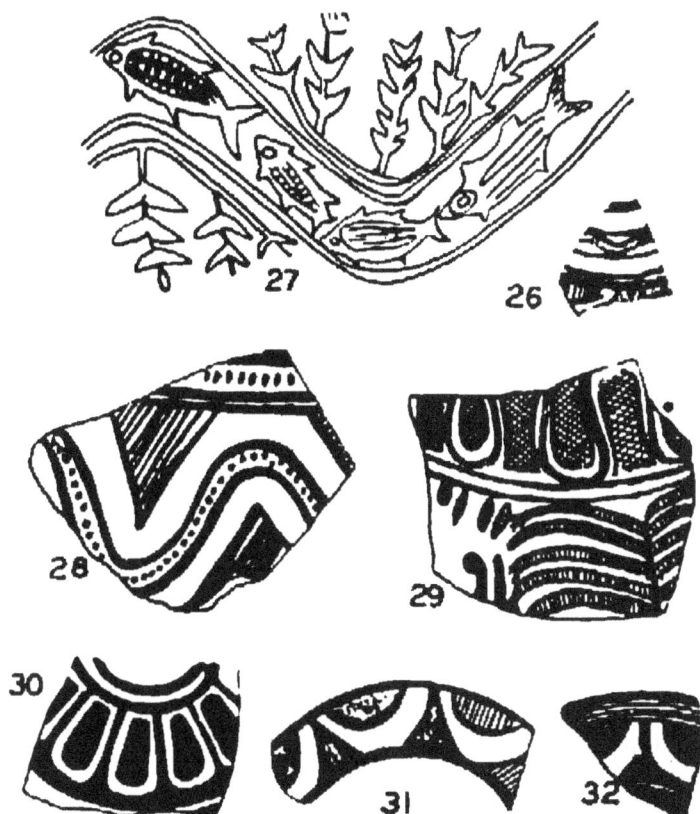

independent decorative element. There must of necessity be many
cases in which we will be unable to distinguish between a degenerated loop pattern and the wavy line motif. For the moment
we may say, somewhat arbitrarily, that those examples bordered
closely by a horizontal line below as well as above may be ruled
out as loop patterns.

In Sumer, and in the adjacent lands directly under its influence, the cylinder seal became the chief medium for the expression of naturalistic pictorialization as early as the Uruk period, and it is from these seals that we get the real key to the riddle of the wavy line used on early pottery. Fig. 27 shows one of the more graphic renderings of this motif found on an Elamite seal attributable to the period of late Uruk or early Jumdat Nasr. Obviously it is a river winding through a valley, bordered on either side, where space permits, by clumps of vegetation. Other examples show stylized mountains in place of vegetation, and still others just a wavy or zigzag line bordered by markings of an indeterminate nature. With the evidence of the seals in mind, one cannot well deny that the wavy line motif seen in Fig. 28 represents a stream flowing through a valley. Fig. 28 is from Shahi-tump mound in British Makran, which is culturally related to Harappa through Kulli, Mehi, and Amri.

Other Harappan examples of this motif will be recognized in the upper border of Fig. 29, as well as in the similar borders seen on Figs. 136 and 142. Fig. 30, which is a "Late Period" design at Harappan sites, seems quite certainly to be an outgrowth of the deep loops used in Fig. 29 in making up the flowing river. Nor can there be any uncertainty as to the close relationship of Figs. 31 and 32 to this design. In the same way Figs. 33, 34, and 35 (the last two from Amri sites) continue the basic principle of alternate rising and pendant projections, creating of the background the regularly waving line which in earlier examples is so clearly a stream. Finally, we have in Figs. 36, 37, and 38 what appears to be the ultimate breakdown of the river pattern. It must be admitted that these last represent a far cry from the realism of Figs. 27 and 28, or even that of Fig. 29. We can only say that in Figs. 36 and 37 the lines are certainly not of the looped class and that both satisfy certain of the requirements of the river pattern in presenting undulating bands closely bordered above and below by horizontals. Fig. 38 is included in the river motif group only under sufferance, for except for wavy lines, which it has in abundance, it has, so far as we are allowed to see, none of the characteristics of this group. Nevertheless, the illusion of water is convincing

whether it is intentional or not, and there is some reason for believing that this mode of decoration used on other early wares
represented water, just as it became the common convention in
Assyrian river-scene reliefs.

Hardly any other of the more complex primitive patterns has
so wide a spread as the river or wavy band. It appears throughout
the region in which we are primarily interested here and is found
even on the prehistoric painted pottery of Kansu Province in
China.[37] Its earliest unquestionable appearance in Iran is in a
graphically depicted example from Persepolis,[38] and it continues
to be used in one variation or another throughout the pottery of

[37] Nils Palmgren, "Kansu Mortuary Urns of the Pan Shan and Ma Chang Groups,"
Palaeontologia Sinica, ser. D. vol. III, fasc. 1, fig. 223, etc.
[38] *Persepolis*, pl. viii, 2.

that site and at related sites in Fars.[29] At Samarra it is only rarely
seen in the flowing, curvilinear style of Fig. 28 or as in the example
cited from Persepolis; but as an angular, zigzag design formed by
alternate upright and pendant triangles as shown in Fig. 39 it is
a common border pattern. At sites of the Halaf period this motif
is certainly present in the multiple wavy bands used as borders and
dividers on bowls. In al-'Ubaid levels it is seen in the wavy lines
and more conventionally in occasional angular versions. It appears
on the Susa I pottery, in the same angular manner as seen at
Samarra, serving more often as a central pattern on the vessel
than as a border. In Sialk II it appears as a free wavy line, and
in Sialk III both in an angular and a snake-like form.[30] Again, in
Fars, we find the curvilinear river pattern freely used on the
wares from Bampur and Khurab in culture levels that appear to
be stylistically about midway between Persepolis and Hisar II
in the case of Bampur, and somewhat later for Khurab.[31] At
Bampur in particular we have a striking parallel to the animal-
bordered step (river) pattern of Susa I, to be discussed below,

and the animal-bordered rivers already noted on early cylinder
seals, for on a pot from that site are mountain goats placed between each drop or rise of the river lines and the horizontal
borders above and below.[32] Still farther to the east, at Shahr-i-
sukhtah in the Helmand Delta, we find examples like those of
Fars among pottery that can be but little later than Persepolis

[29] See, for example, Tal-i-pir, *Reconn.*, pl. xxix, vi. 25.
[30] *Sialk*, pls. I, B, D; lxxi, S. 1820; lxvi, S. 1766.
[31] *Reconn.*, pl. viii, A. 195, etc.; pl. xiii, Khur. B. ii. 202.
[32] *Ibid.*, pl. xiv, Bam. A. 162.

itself.[32] In Tepe Hisar IIA we have the angular form of this
motif as well as remnants of the curvilinear form.[34] In Hisar IIB
we have as a common border the design reproduced in Fig. 40,
which one will recognize as basically the same as the two Amri
examples Figs. 34 and 35. At Ja'farabad near Susa we have again
a clearly recognizable river pattern among finds comparable to
Musyan.[35] And finally, among the Susa II vessels we have parallel
wavy lines between horizontals that must be a survival of this
same pattern.

Fig. 38 with its broad band of wavy lines may be compared
with the vertical streamers so popular in Sialk III and Hisar I
and II, and more especially with the horizontal streamers of
Susa I which occur in separated panels just as seems to be indicated by the vertical dividing line of Fig. 38. Attention should
also be called to the band of wavy lines on the Samarra specimen,
Fig. 58, and particularly to the lines on the vessel from Tepe
Gawra XII, on which is depicted a landscape of valley and river,
hunter and quarry.[36]

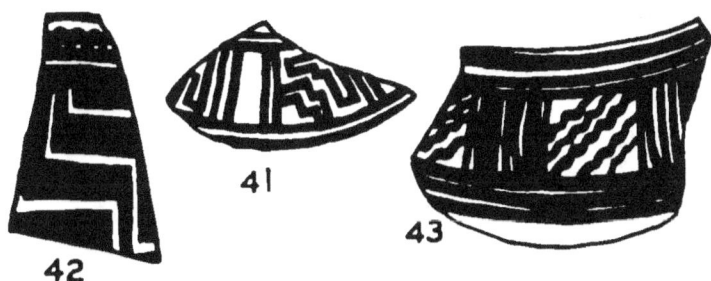

41

42

43

The so-called step motif (Figs. 41-3) is usually considered as a
separate decorative element. The pattern as such does not concern
Harappa directly since no Harappan examples of it have yet been
found; but it does concern Harappa indirectly through Amri
(Figs. 41-3) and its related Baluchi cultures. The traditional

[32] Inn. Asia, III, pl. cxiii, S.S. 024.   [34] Hissar, pl. xxi, H 4743; pl. xxii, H 4676.
[35] Del. en Perse, xx, fig. 20, 10.
[36] E. A. Speiser in Bull. A.I.I.A.A., v, p. 5 assigns the vessel to Gawra XV. In a
recent verbal communication he gave its level as Gawra XII, reconfirming his attribution
in Bull. A.S.O.R., no. 64, pp. 8-9.

home of the step pattern is Susa I, though it appears earlier at Tal-i-regi (Khusu) and Tal-i-skau in Fars among designs of a developed Persepolis style,[37] and earlier still in sporadic examples from Sialk I.[38] At Susa we see it used both as a true step with horizontal tread and vertical riser, and as a zigzag series of lines extending straight downward from the upper portion or lip of the vessel. Actually the two are but variations of one motif and that motif is the river pattern. We have already noted the similarity between the irregular horizontal wavy (river) lines of Harappa and the vertical bands of wavy lines from Hisar I and II and Sialk III. What was not made clear at that point was that at Hisar and Sialk these wavy streamers are interchangeable with zigzag ones—exactly like those of Susa I—and that the two are

44

45

but variations of one motif. And it is now certainly clear that the horizontal river pattern can as well be angular as curvilinear. Thus one can see that a step pattern may only be an angular form of the river pattern diverted from its usual horizontal direction. Nor need we be disturbed by the multiplicity of lines in a step pattern when we remember the large number of curvilinear lines in some of the river patterns of Susa I.[39]

[37] *Perris*, pl. xxvi. 15, 19, 35; pl. xxviii. 32. Seen also in Gawra XIII: *Bull. A.S.O.R.*, no. 66, fig. 7.

[38] *Sialk*, pl. xlii, D, 10.　　　　　　　　　　[39] *Del. en Perse*, xiii, pl. xxii, 8, 9.

The proof that the step pattern and the river pattern are but variants of one motif comes also from Susa I. The step shown in the Susian example, Fig. 44, has springing from it two stylized plant stalks, above and below the stepped lines. Look now at the vegetation bordering the river in Fig. 27 and the identity of idea will at once be apparent. The same convention is repeated in the bold zigzag encircling the Susian beaker shown in Fig. 45, where from at least two sections of the band other plant stalks sprout upward, away from the path of the line. That these were actually serving as an identification for the motif in question is assured by the fact that here the artist felt it necessary to disregard his typically Susian love of symmetry in order to introduce these additions. Other Susian examples exist in which the head of a

bighorn sheep emerges from the step in place of plant stalks, in exactly the same relation as the animals bordering the river scenes in the early cylinder seals.[19]

The correlation of the step with the river pattern is an interesting example of two nominally distinct patterns springing from one source—patterns that were used as independent decorative

[19] See the example from Musyan, *Del. en Perse*, viii, fig. 110. The identification of the zigzag band of fig. 45 as a river pattern conflicts with Frankfort's belief in its origination as an imitation of leather-working technique. Actually both may be true. If this is so, we can only assume that by the time of Susa I the pattern had ceased to be imitative of leather work and had become wholly identified with the river motif, for it is impossible now to believe that the Susians were still dependent on leather in the light of the ancient and earlier history of pottery on the Iranian plateau. I cannot agree with Pézard that the zigzag band represents mountains (*Studies*, pp. 29-32), or with Tuscanne's belief that the step and zigzag are serpent symbols (*Del. en Perse*, XII, pp. 155. et seq.).

motifs within a given culture level, yet understood at the time of use in their true light. And there seems little doubt that the meaning of the step symbol was understood long after the time of Susa I. One need only look at the fluid aspect of the stepped lines in the Amri example, Fig. 43, to feel assured of this. Still more explicit is the manner in which the stag on the even later vase from Nal, Fig. 46, emerges from the angular border, in exactly the same relationship to the design as a whole as the stags and plants of the Susa I river patterns. And on a sherd from Susa II we see a wholly realistic version wherein a fish is used to mark clearly the course of the stream."

Fig. 47 represents an example of the step pattern from Ram-rud, in the Helmand Delta, on the very edge of the Indo-Baluchi sphere of influence, which helps mark the path by which this motif spread from Fars to the east. It is uncertain whether or not we may consider the continuous stepped border so popular at Samarra as a member of this same group. It is possible, but so far we lack the proof. Other equally obscure geometrical designs doubtless had as realistic an origin, but we lack the clues through which they may be identified.

IV

Lozenge pattern. The ubiquitous lozenge appears in Harappan designs usually in horizontal rows as a border pattern (Figs. 48, 78-81). Whether or not this pattern originally developed from interlacing wavy lines, and is thus related to the river pattern, is a question that cannot be answered in the present state of our knowledge of early pottery designs. However, that the two are related seems unlikely when we see the lozenge and the curvilinear and angular river pattern used together in the same culture levels, each as a distinctly different pattern, without one ever taking on the attributes of the other.

A single example (Fig. 49) exists in which rows of connected lozenges are used as an all-over pattern. This has a significant parallel in a bowl from Sialk II." More interesting still is the repeated use of connected lozenges as an all-over pattern in the

⁴¹ *Del. en Perse*, xiii, fig. 179.　　　⁴² *Sialk*, pl. xlvi, S. 1747.

pottery of the Halaf period." These, it should be noted, are closer in spirit to the Harappan specimen than the more restrained treatment seen at Sialk.

The unconnected lozenges seen on such Harappan pieces as Figs. 108, 155, and 156 are explicable as unattached and conventionalized leaf patterns. Fig. 101, though tentatively placed in another group, may also belong in this same class.

V

Triangle patterns. Triangles as such, unassociated with those growing out of the grid pattern," are relatively rare at Harappan sites. This is understandable when we consider the propensity of the Harappans for curvilinear design. Those specimens that

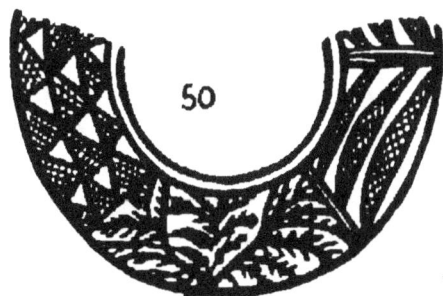

do appear may be considered as survivals of an ancient and widespread tradition. Fig. 50 represents the triangle motif combined with curvilinear, naturalistic designs painted on the shoulder of a pot from Mohenjo-daro." Even in this example there is some question as to whether it may not be an outgrowth of experimentation with the diagonally cut grids to be discussed later.

** *Arpachiyah*, figs. 51, 2; 50, 4; 66, 1; 67, 1; etc.   ** See below, pp. 58-61.
** Triangles identical in design and disposition with those of fig. 50 appear in *Jemdet Nasr*, pl. lxviii, 1, 3; pl. lxxviii, 1.

There is one pattern based on triangles which though not actually found so far at Harappan sites can be predicted with a fair degree of certainty as being among future Harappan finds. Its path from Samarra in Mesopotamia into Baluchistan is clearly marked, and its presence among the designs of Amri and Jhukar bring it directly into the valley of the Indus. This is the pattern illustrated by the Samarra sherd, Fig. 51, in which contiguous upright and inverted triangles are individually differentiated by diagonal hatching sloping alternately right and left. Painted versions of this pattern are rare. Besides those from Samarra, we have it on small vases from Susa I,[46] on a sherd from Giyan V,[47] and very much later, in Early Dynastic times, on sherds of Nineveh V.[48] However, it is more common to find it incised on pottery or stone. As such it appears over an amazingly wide area, from Predynastic Egypt and Early Minoan Crete to western Baluchistan on the borders of Afghanistan.[49] There is every probability that this incised pattern is an imitation of a common weave in matting. As such, its presence in such distant and faintly related areas as Egypt or Crete is easily understandable. With the incised specimens from Mesopotamia and southern Iran there does seem to be a close interrelationship, one closer than could be explained by isolated imitations of the same basic weave. The consistency with which it is used on stone, or dark gray pottery resembling stone, its association with certain other distinct motifs such as the "house façade" with its sagging lintel, and its restriction largely to vessels of one flat-bottomed type point to a certain unity of tradition and craft technique, the explanation for which is not wholly clear as yet. Nevertheless, the presence of the sagging or straight lintel of the "house

---

[46] *Del. en Perse,* xiii, pl. xix, 1; pl. xxi, 7.   [47] *Giyan,* pl. 43, top left.
[48] *Nineveh, 1931-2,* pl. liv, 5.
[49] Egypt: W. M. F. Petrie, *Abydos* (London, 1902), pt. i, pl. liii. Crete: H. G. Spearing, *Childhood of Art* (London, 1930), ii, fig. 305. Mesopotamia: numerous examples, only one of which (from Mari) need be given here, *Syria,* xvi, pl. xxvii, 3. Susa: *Del. en Perse,* xiii, fig. 116. Iran: (either displaying the triangle pattern or other incised designs associated with it). *Reconn.,* pl. vi, Kai. 019; Khur. F. i. 263; Bam. A. 161; pl. viii, A. 142; A. 140; A. 141; A. 34; A. 365; pl. ix, Bam. Surf. 473; *Iran. Asia,* ii, p. 968, R.R. VII. 02-5; iii, pl. cxiii, R.R. VII. 01; pl. cxv, R.R. VII. 015. Baluchistan: *Gedrosia,* pl. xiii, Sh. T. iii. 9.

[44]

façade" motif, with which our triangles are almost invariably associated, among the painted designs of such early sites as Susa I, Tal-i-skau in Fars, and Ram-rud in the Helmand Delta points with some certainty to highland Iran as the point of origin for this particular association of architectural patterns.[10]

The incised versions, however, are of no direct concern in so far as the Indus Valley is concerned.[11] In painted wares we find our triangular pattern perfectly executed in the later culture of Jhukar,[12] and from an Amri site we have the fragment illustrated in Fig. 52. Though the latter is not complete, it appears to be the same pattern of alternately hatched, opposed triangles just discussed. At Amri itself we have the pattern illustrated in Fig. 53

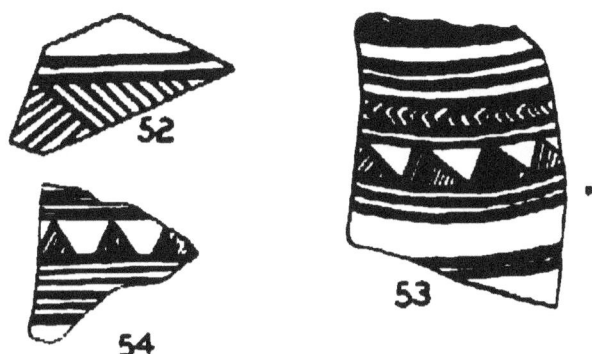

52

53

54

which is essentially the same, so far as it goes, as the pattern under discussion. Opposed triangles are there; all that is lacking is the oblique hatching of the pendant row. Finally, from Mohenjo-daro we have Fig. 54, the separation of whose triangles —thus eliminating the pendant or opposed row—shows a design more degenerated than that of the Amri example Fig. 53.

The pattern of opposed triangles with alternate diagonal hatching in painted pottery quite certainly is inspired by the weaves

[10] *Dél. en Perse,* XIII, pl. III, 2; pl. XIX, 4; *Persis,* pl. XXIV, 1, 6; *Ina. Ania.* III, pl. cxiii, R.R. XVII. 01.

[11] One clearly related specimen, in carved steatite with a somewhat different weave, comes from Mohenjo-daro. However, this is so closely related to one from Susa (G. Contenau, *Manuel d'Archéologie Orientale,* I, fig. 169) and so foreign in technique to Harappa as a whole that it must be considered as a foreign importation. For a comparison of the two, see Ernest Mackay in *Antiquity,* VI, no. 23 (Sept., 1932), pp. 356-7.

[12] *A.R.A.S.J.,* 1927-28, pl. XXX, 9; listed there as being of the Gupta period.

of basketry or matting, just as were the incised examples discussed earlier. There are occasions, however, when the striking zigzag effect of the design became confused, in the minds of certain Iranian potters, with the river pattern with its alternating, but separate, opposed triangles.[1] In these few instances the combination of the two motifs seems fortuitous and does not necessarily imply a common origin.

VI

Sigma and chevron designs. Since both the sigma and chevron pattern spring from the same natural concept, they will be discussed here under one joint heading. In so far as is possible they will be treated separately within this subdivision.

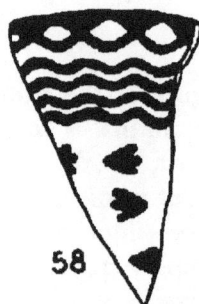

Considering first the sigma, we find that the only example from a Harappan site is that illustrated in Fig. 55. At Amri sites, however, it is a very popular border pattern, the figures facing as often to the left (Fig. 56) as to the right. Looking now to the

[1] *Reconn.*, pl. xv, 1. ii 203 (painted—from Khurab burial site): pl. xx, B11. 3 (incised—from Bijnabad).

west, we find the pattern at Persepolis, Samarra, Nineveh 2b (Halaf period), Susa I, Giyan V, Musyan, at a number of sites in Fars, Iranian Makran and the Helmand Delta (Fig. 57), and at Shahi-tump mound in British Makran. And there are among the specimens from the sites enumerated sufficiently clear gradations to show that the angular form of Fig. 56 and the cursive forms of Figs. 55 and 57 are but different ways of showing the same thing.

One cannot but be impressed by the feeling of motion and flight brought up by the figures in Fig. 57. Returning to Samarra, one sees in the more common manner of rendering at that site much the same type of representation in Fig. 58; and in

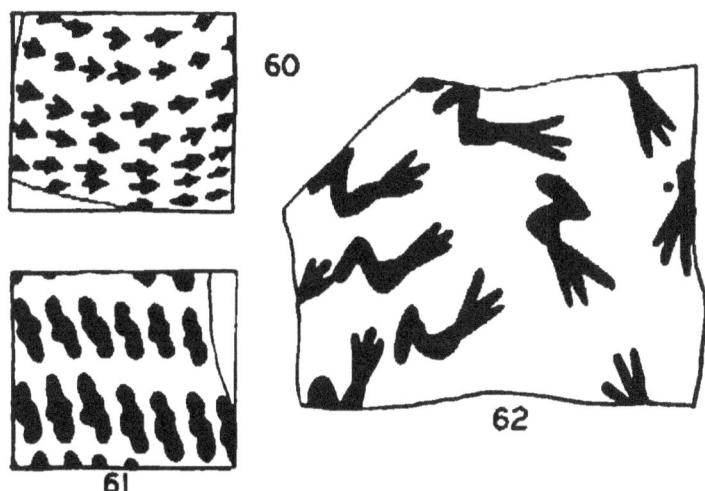

60

61

62

Fig. 59, also from Samarra, one is confirmed in the opinion that the symbol represents a flying creature of some sort. In the later site, Musyan, the specimens illustrated in Figs. 60 and 61 show an interesting though somewhat degenerated survival of the forms seen in Figs. 58 and 59.[54] Complete confirmation for the impression of flight is had by returning again to Samarra, for in Fig. 62 from that site the figures are represented in what must

[54] For a parallel to fig. 58 from al-'Ubaid times see *Arpachiyah*, fig. 77, 25. Seen also in Sialk II, *Sialk*, pl. xlvi, S 1736. The symbols in fig. 60 cannot be considered as arrowheads since the leaf-shaped point was the form both for Musyan and Susa.

have been their true naturalistic form. Here they emerge as clearly defined birds which in other examples had been symbolized simply by wings, tail, and body.

In case the connection between the sigma and Fig. 62 seems an unjustified assumption, a glance at the more elaborate forms will serve as a confirmation of their relationship. Fig. 63 from Giyan V shows a row of connected birds flying upward toward the rim of the vessel.[53] In certain Susian examples, identical birds, complete and each separate from the other, are shown in horizontal rows.[54] The Susian examples in particular show the basic sigma shape of the design as a whole. From the somewhat later site, Khazinah, we have Fig. 64, in which the bird is highly stylized and conventionalized, approaching again the purely sym-

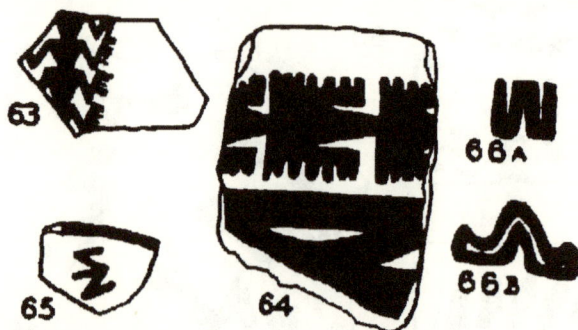

bolic form seen in the simple sigma. Finally, from Tal-i-regi (Khusu) in Fars comes the form illustrated in Fig. 65 in which the bird is reduced to its basic skeleton of body, wings, and head.[57]

In looking at the outline of the birds in Fig. 63 one could argue with reason that they should be correlated not with a

---

[53] More clearly represented by *Del. en Perse*, VIII, fig. 203 from Khazinah. These should not be confused with the so-called human figures of Khazinah shown in *ibid.*, figs. 262-4, for fundamental differences separate the two. The design from Musyan *ibid.*, fig. 261, described there as humans, must, in the light of *ibid.*, fig. 203, and the Giyan example cited above, be interpreted as birds.

[54] *Del. en Perse*, XIII, pl. XXI, 9; pl. XXII, 5.

[57] For the true sigma in its most elemental feathered form see the example from Khurab shown in *Reconn.*, pl. XIV, Khur. B. ii. 157; similarly feathered three- and five-armed "sigmas" come from Damin, pl. XII, Dmn. B. 121 and 112.

[48]

sigma with its four parts but with a zigzag line of six parts. Exactly that variation was used on a few of the Susa I specimens, in conjunction with the more customary sigma figures." It appears, however, to have been a short-lived form and one that did not travel beyond Susa I. We must believe, then, that the six possible basic lines obtainable on breaking down figures such as those of Fig. 63 represent a naturalistic elaboration of the simpler four-line figure by which birds in flight are symbolized at so many places in the Ancient East.

The formalized sigma from Baluchistan, Fig. 66, A, is a common form of the bird at both Kulli and Mehi, where it is shown among pipal leaves or in the air above large quadrupeds. The yoke-shaped symbol from Nal, Fig. 66, B, is probably a further conventionalization of the bird-sigma, though unlike others of Baluchistan and the Indus Valley it is the central figure

of a given design rather than an embellishment to a naturalistic scene.

Turning now to the chevron pattern, Fig. 67 and the smaller members of Figs. 78, 132, and 133 are the only Harappan specimens showing the chevron in its simple form. Amri, on the other hand, used the pattern in a more generous, though still sparing, fashion. The Amri example, Fig. 53, shows it in its conventional form, and Fig. 68 illustrates a variant, common throughout Iran and Mesopotamia as well. In one or both of these forms it is almost universally represented among the prehistoric culture levels of Iran and Mesopotamia. Fig. 69 shows the formalized

** Del. en Perse, xiii, pl. xvii, 3.

version as seen at Samarra, and Fig. 70 from Hisar IA shows the compact and more common rendering. Similar examples come from sites of Halaf and al-'Ubaid culture, and regularly in highland Iran and Baluchistan.

Even a cursory examination will show that the chevron is also a member of the flying-bird group. Fig. 71 from Susa I shows the feather patterns just as we have seen them in Figs. 63 and 64,[59] and other examples from the even older Samarra period show similar feathered chevrons, though here the feathers pro-

71

72

73

74

75

ject from the inner edges."[60] Further confirmation comes from the al-'Ubaid period where symbols like those of Fig. 58, which have already been identified as birds, are used together, and intermixed with, plain chevrons."[61] Fig. 72 from Deh-bid in Fars shows the chevron in its completely naturalistic form, found among pottery comparable to that of Persepolis. This last example must be compared with the naturalistically-drawn bird from Persepolis in which the solid portions of the wings are shown in

[59] For comparison with fig. 76 see Dél. en Perse, XIII, pl. xvi, 5.

[60] Arpachiyah, fig. 77, 24.

[61] Ibid., fig. 77, 25.

rounded form.[42] Such wing form relates to the flight pattern from Musyan seen in Fig. 73 as well as to a similar pattern from Hisar IC.[44] A strikingly similar survival of the Deh-bid birds (Fig. 72) comes from Periano-ghundai in northern Baluchistan, illustrated in Fig. 74.

Figs. 75 and 76 from Susa I are understandable now as stylized birds, though without the examples already cited, and the many more that cannot be treated here, they might be taken as stylized stag heads. They are, for that matter, but simplified forms of the figures seen in Figs. 63 and 64. Figs. 75 and 76 also serve

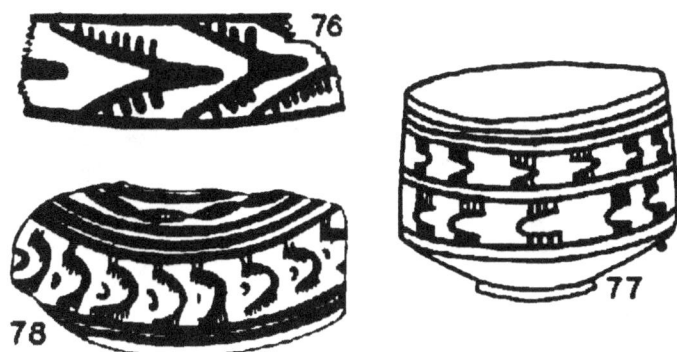

to identify the symbols on the example from Nal, Fig. 77. The latter, in preserving more perfectly the ancient form of the symbol, serves to identify its more corrupted, though presumably earlier, Harappan counterpart, Fig. 78. This final Harappan version of the chevron or flying-bird pattern has lost almost all of the naturalistic appearance of the earlier specimens, yet the necessary members are all present, albeit inaccurately placed, and the essential chevron form is preserved, along with the feather lines. Whether or not the Harappans still understand the symbolism of this particular pattern is doubtful. It is quite prob-

[42] *Persepolis*, pl. xvi, 1.
[44] *Hisar*, pl. 11, H 4742. For chevron and heart-shaped figures used together see *Arpachiyah*, fig. 77, 16 (al-'Ubaid period); also for the al-'Ubaid period see the specimen from Gawra XIII in *Bull. A.S.O.R.*, no. 66, fig. 7, where curvilinear line of flight should be compared with those from Khazinah, *Del. en. Perse*, viii, figs. 199-200. Similar heart-shaped figures are found in the early Iranian culture exposed at Tal-i-Bakun (Madavan) in Fars (*Perse*, pl. xxii, 51).

able that they did not, for in adding the upward-extending lines at the top to give connection with the parallels above as well as below, they seem to be repeating one of the features of an earlier, traditional pattern rather than an understood symbol. Had they known the true meaning, the connection above and below would not have been necessary, since in earlier examples it is merely the accidental result of fitting a bird figure as a decoration between two horizontal lines. Nevertheless, some connection between the plain and the feathered chevron seems still to have been recognized, since we see them used alternately in this example.

VII

Comb motif. A considerable number of painted sherds from Mohenjo-daro—but from no other Harappan site—feature the comb motif or "comb animal" so commonly found on the interiors

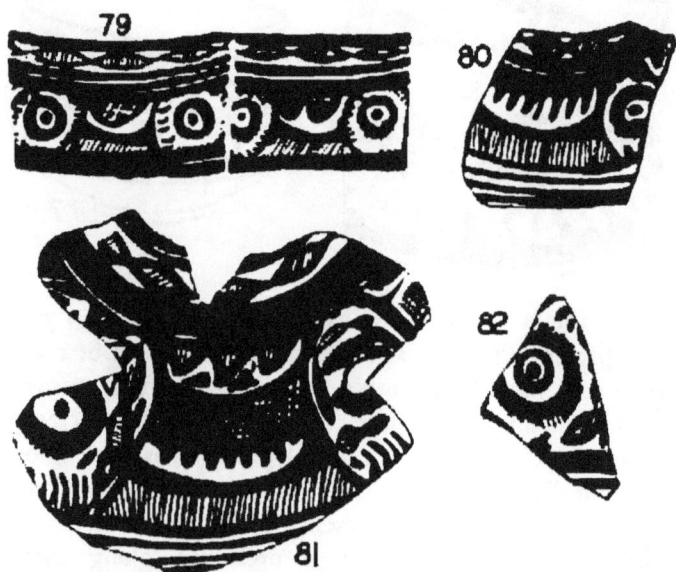

of bowls from Susa I. It is of interest that very little effort is made toward an animalistic representation, the heads of the two Harappan examples shown in Fig. 79 being the only ones featuring the usual downward slant seen in the foreign examples, Figs. 84 and 85. The head on Fig. 80 is shown by a terminal bulbousness, while that of Fig. 81 does not seem to be accentuated in any way. A definite note of naturalism can be seen, however, in Fig. 81, where the upper body is crosshatched in the same manner as in some of the more naturalistic Harappan animals (cf. Fig. 156, etc.). The introduction of an upper body as seen here is a curious feature for which there is a precedent in the doublebodied combs of the Nehavand region—and there only—as illustrated in Fig. 85. The essential feature of the Indian upper body is a series of hatched loops (one and two in Fig. 79), or a series of pendant solid blobs (Fig. 80), above the back of the comb proper. Fig. 81 portrays both styles—the solid loops above the lower body of the comb and the hatched loops above the upper body.

The fine horizontal projecting lines seen on the legs in the two examples in Fig. 79 are not a part of the figure proper but belong to the rayed circle with which the comb motif of Mohenjodaro and Baluchistan is always associated. Its most elaborate Harappan form is seen in Fig. 82. Exactly this pattern is found in Halaf culture levels, but more often it takes there the form of a center dot surrounded successively by a circle and a ring of dots.[44] An example similar to the latter comes from Susa I,[45] while groups of concentric rings are common in the ware of Susa II. At Hisar in levels IB and IC it appears in a number of variations within the circle made by the curving horns of a mountain goat. It is of particular interest to see that there it is interchangeable, and apparently synonymous, with the six- and eight-armed pommée cross.[46] This relates it not only to the Persepolitan culture, but the clear emergence of the six- or eight-armed cross or star in Sumer into an astral symbol would also suggest a similar meaning here. Even without this suggestive connection, one would be tempted to call the figure as seen in Figs. 79-82 a sun symbol.

[44] *Halaf*, color pl. i, 1; *Arpachiyah*, fig. 67, 2. The latter is also found in Harappan pottery, but with plant rather than animal forms; see *Sind*, pl. xxvi, 5.
[45] *Del. en Perse*, xiii, pl. v, 3.   [46] *Infra.*, fig. 152.

To return to the comb motif itself, we have from an Amri site the example shown in Fig. 83, and from Mehi in Baluchistan two others similarly placed on a single vessel.[67] The similarity between these of Amri and Fig. 84, C, from Susa I is perfectly clear.

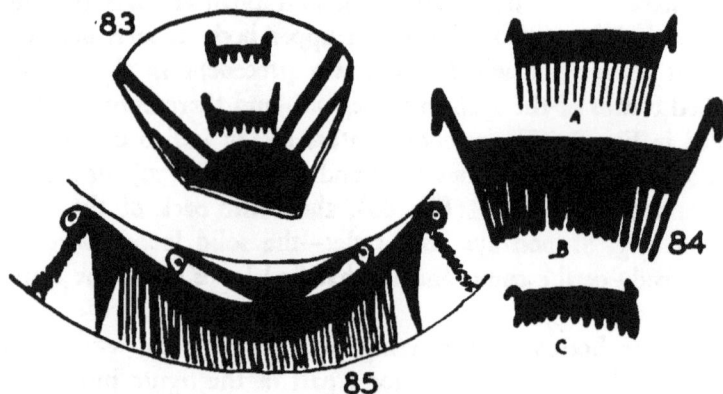

In Susa I the comb is the most common of all the decorative motifs other than the conventional repeat patterns used as borders. Fig. 84 shows it in some of its commoner Susian forms, while Fig. 85 shows its development as seen in Giyan IV, a period which is contemporary with, or even later than, Susa II.[68] Particular attention should be given to the presence of an upper body, or comb back, relating this form to the specimens of Mohenjo-daro.

The very limited distribution of the "comb animal" is of interest here. It is common in Susa I and in the late cultures of the Giyan-Nehavand region, and we have already noted its presence in Baluchistan and along the Indus. Others are found only in one spot—at Sialk in Central Iran (Fig. 88); these will be discussed below. No true "combs" are known in Mesopotamia; certain specimens from the Halaf levels of Arpachiyah and Tepe

[67] *Gedrosia*, pl. xxx, Mehi. II. 4. 5. See the two similar specimens from Kulli, placed side by side, with a "sun symbol" between: pl. xxiii, Kul. V. vii. 2 (illustrated upside down).

[68] *Del. en Perse*, xvi, fig. 65 shows the survival of the comb body, without the teeth, on an early Elamite cylinder seal.

Gawra may possibly belong to this class, but their certain relationship to an insect-like representation from Tell Halaf itself makes this most uncertain.[69] Obviously, there is a considerable evolutionary period, from which we have no examples, separating the Susa I and Giyan IV renderings.

The comb motif is usually thought of as being a stylization and conventionalization of an eagle, or more often, of a long-haired quadruped, probably a mountain sheep or goat. That it represents one of the larger horned quadrupeds rather than a bird is indicated first by its constant association at Mohenjo-daro and in Baluchistan with the "sun" symbol which, as has been pointed out above, is in one form or another an almost universal attribute of the large-horned quadrupeds on the earlier painted wares of Iran and Mesopotamia. Even more conclusive evidence comes from Sialk II where we have the mountain goat depicted in the manner seen in Fig. 86. From this we have the logical

Sialk II simplification shown in Fig. 87, used there as an all-over pattern. We need now only the elimination of the bottom border to have a true "comb animal," and in that same Sialk level we see, in Fig. 88, that exactly that final step in conventionalization did take place.[70] There can be little doubt that the "comb animal"

[69] *Arpachiyah*, fig. 78, 28; *Gawra*, pl. lxxii, 1; *Halaf*, pl. liii, 1.

[70] An example from the Shahi-tump burials (*Gedrosia*, pl. xvii, Sh. T. vi. 4. 2) shows what must have been an alternative step in the development, the lower border having been abandoned while the head and horns still remain.

came into being through steps such as have just been outlined.
It is of interest that the teeth of the comb do not represent long
hair, but are the result of the practice of showing the bodies of
larger animals by hatching within bordering lines. This manner
of rendering (hatching) was one of widespread popularity, as
will be pointed out in greater detail under the heading *Animal
designs.*

VIII

Cross motif. The Harappan cross motif, illustrated by Fig. 89,
and its more elaborate Amri counterpart, Fig. 90, quite probably
had their origin in the popular Maltese cross of Lower Mesopotamia and Iran.[71] Figs. 89 and 90 both display the essential
characteristics of right-angle radiating arms springing from an
enclosed or separated area in the center. Fig. 91, from Tal-i-regi

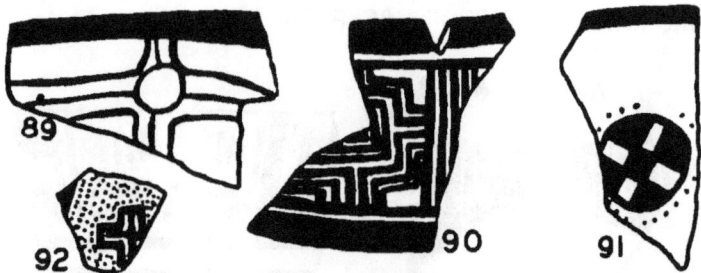

(Khusu) in Fars, shows the cruciform pattern more clearly than
the previously illustrated specimens,[72] while Fig. 92 from that
same site shows a variation of the pattern relating particularly to
the Harappan specimen, Fig. 89, by means of the central line

[71] Strangely enough the Maltese cross, so popular in Iran and Mesopotamia, does not
appear on Harappan ware. There can be little doubt that the Maltese cross sprang from
the balanced geometrical grouping of four stags around a central hub, as we see it in
Samarra, abb. 23, nr. 23, which in turn may have come from the less stylized arrangement of *Samarra*, abb. 20, nr. 20. At Tal-i-regi (Khusu) in Fars, as illustrated in *Persis*,
pl. xxv, 53, the stag has almost ceased to be recognizable, prominence being given largely
to the cross-like bodies. At Musyan (*Del. en Perse*, viii, fig. 177) we have further examples
showing the progress of simplification where only the conventionalized antlers remain
to show its origin. The Maltese cross in various parts of Iran and Elam, early and late,
often retained serrated or pronged outer edges as faint reminders of their naturalistic
origin (*Persepolis*, pl. xxii; *Inn. Asia*, iii, pl. cxiii, Md. (R.R.) II. 03; *Reconn.*, pl. xiii,
Khur. B. ii. 200; *Persian Art*, iv, pl. 3, C).
[72] Occurring also at Persepolis: *O.I.C.*, 21 fig. 91.

or cross within the outer border.[72] It is of interest that this very common western figure should have but few representatives in Harappan culture, and those so sketchily done.

IX

Grid patterns. One of the most characteristic features of the painted pottery of Harappan sites is its decided preference for repeat patterns built upon the variations and elaborations to be had from a grid of vertical and horizontal lines. The introduction of diagonal lines makes possible various combinations of triangles, while the division of the squares into arcs opens up a field of curvilinear patterns based upon the same rectilinear foundation. It is of particular interest that we find among the ancient cultures of the west only one in which there is a similarly marked preference for this type of pattern: namely, Tell Halaf. We see there the same, or even greater, mastery of the technique as in India, with many points of similarity in detail and in spirit. Certain

93 94 95

variations on this basic pattern also enjoyed some popularity in Sialk III and to an even lesser extent in other, scattered western fabrics, as will be pointed out below.

(Checker pattern). The most elemental of the grid patterns is the checker, illustrated in Figs. 93-5, 114, 135, and 142. The alternate squares are demarked by crosshatching, with only two (Figs. 114, 142) having the checkers filled with solid color. The light squares in Figs. 94 and 95 illustrate by their fillers of dot

[72] Also in Susa I: *Dél. en Perse.* i, pl. xix, 8.

and circle or short oblique strokes the usual avoidance of undecorated fields.

It is only natural that so simple a design should be found, as
it is, among all the prehistoric culture levels of Mesopotamia
and Elam, as well as at many of the less clearly understood
chalcolithic sites of highland Iran. It appears even among the
limited repertoire of designs possessed by Anau I. Among the
later western cultures, Jumdat Nasr, which is considered as contemporary with the earliest phase of Mohenjo-daro, uses the
checker patterns most extensively.

(Triangle patterns). The most common Harappan repeat pattern based on triangles is that illustrated by the diagram, Fig. 96. It

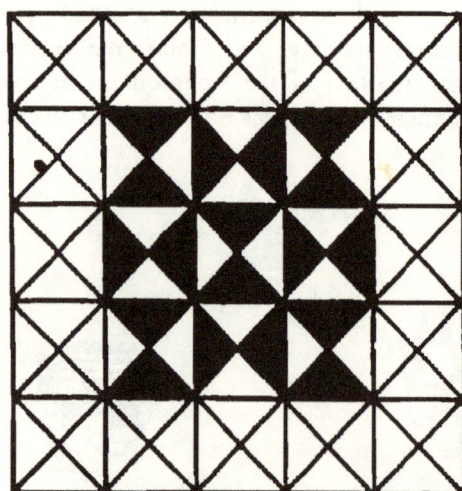

96

97

98

is wholly dependent on the grid in its composition, and though
basically simple it gives a rich effect when used as a filler over
large areas (Figs. 97 and 98). As one would expect, it is found
elsewhere only at those places where grid patterns were favored.
Samarra shows a related specimen in the single row of alternating
upright and horizontal opposed triangles.[74] Musyan yields us one

[74] *Samarra*, abb. 16a, nr. 218. See also the more elaborate triangle pattern in abb. 23,
nr. 23.

fragmentary example,[75] but it is only in Halaf strata and in Sialk III that it is as fully developed as in Harappan sites.[76] Another true example from Iran is seen in a single sherd from Tal-i-skau in Fars.[77]

A simplification of this motif is that built upon the plan illustrated in Fig. 99. By its very nature it is limited to a single row of ornament, which is the way we see it in Fig. 100, and more graphically on the left in Fig. 112. Fig. 101 introduces a

99

100

101

filler between the pairs of triangles which is a combination of the lines of Fig. 100 and the dotted circle of Fig. 112.

There is some doubt as to whether or not we can consider this pattern (Fig. 99) a direct outgrowth of the grid. A very similar design is found throughout Mesopotamian and Iranian cultures arising from diagonal lines passed between the corners of separate squares or rectangles. The squares thus treated appear also in horizontal rows but are separated, often widely, by vertical straight or wavy lines. Unlike the Harappan specimens

[75] *Del. en Perse*, viii, fig. 155.
[76] *Arpachiyah*, fig. 78, 8. *Sialk*, pl. lxxiv, S. 1691. For the use of the bare grid from which this design is derived see the Halaf specimen from Gawra in *Bull. A.S.O.R.*, no. 65, fig. 3.
[77] *Persis*, pl. xxviii, 33.

the triangles accentuated by solid color are usually those which are horizontally contiguous—tip to tip—rather than vertical pairs as in Figs. 99-101.[78] The Harappan specimens are in all probability built on this same foundation, though the influence of the grid technique can be seen in the close proximity of the pairs to each other and the general orderliness of their arrangement.

102

103

104

106

107

105

108

109

An even simpler pattern is that in which a grid is cut by parallel diagonal lines. Accentuation of every other half of the bisected squares gives a row, or rows, of uniformly arranged

[78] This is sometimes referred to as the "double axe" pattern. Though there is a similarity, this is such an elemental and natural recourse as a horizontal filler that the likeness is in all probability fortuitous.

triangles. Thus far this has not been found on Harappan sherds, but its presence among the Amri designs,[19] and at numerous western sites,[80] would lead one to expect it among future Harappan finds.

(Intersecting-circle patterns). The most common of all the geometrical patterns on Harappan pottery are those based on circles interlacing in the manner illustrated by Fig. 102. Fig. 103 shows it in its purest form. Here again, we see the typical *horror vacui* of the Harappan decorators in the crosshatch filler within the intersecting segments. Figs. 104, 124, and 125 show the pattern in more conventionalized form, while Figs. 105 and 122 show the complete breakdown of the pattern, recognizable only through the medium of Fig. 10. In Fig. 106 we have the circle

110

111

112

113

114

motif used as a border, and in Figs. 107-9 we see its merger with plant forms or at least forms that are recognizable as plants under other circumstances.

Other patterns are possible on this same framework by accentuating one or another of the enclosed areas. Treatment such

[19] *Sind*, pl. xxxix, 8.
[80] *Turkestan*, fig. 71; *Persepolis*, pl. xxii; *Arpachiyah*, pls. xiv, xv, etc.; *Giyan*, pl. 45; *Del. en Perse*, viii, figs. 160-3, etc.

as is illustrated by the diagram, Fig. 110, gives rise to what Mackay calls the "stretched hide" motif.[61] This is the most common of all the variations on the intersecting-circle pattern. The typical examples shown in Figs. 111-13 illustrate the degree of conventionalization to which it has been brought in its use as a filler for large spaces, while Fig. 114[62] shows the accentuated areas filled with the familiar checker pattern.

Accentuation of other areas of the intersecting-circle pattern gives the design illustrated by Fig. 115. Few of the Harappan examples show the regularity of Fig. 116. Drawn with little

116

115
117

attention to the skeleton from which they are derived, specimens such as Fig. 117 tend to lose their identity as evenly radiating ellipses and in some cases become indistinguishable from plant forms.

In looking for material comparable to the Harappan intersecting circles, we must rule out the Baluchistan examples, for they are either obvious Harappan products or pieces made within the Harappan sphere of influence. Beyond eastern Baluchistan we have absolutely no similar designs except among the products of one culture, Halaf. From the late Halaf levels of Chagar Bazar, for example, we have a series of intersecting circles, like Fig. 103, that if seen as a design alone could well be taken for Harappan.[63] Parallels to the design of Fig. 110 exist in abundance

[61] *M-d,* p. 337.
[62] For identical examples from Amri and Baluchistan see *Sind,* pl. xviii, 6 and *Gedrosia,* pl. xxiv, Tik. N. 5.
[63] *Chagar Bazar,* pl. ii, 2.

among the finds of the Halaf period. Naturally, the design on Fig. 115, which is the reverse of Fig. 110, exists there as well, and one example from Chagar Bazar, with its heavily outlined leaves and hatched centers, could easily be mistaken for Harappan work.[64]

(Contiguous-circle pattern). Rare among Harappan finds, but not unique, is the pattern illustrated in Fig. 118, based on an understood grid in which are rows of contiguous circles in the manner illustrated by Fig. 119. Fig. 120 shows it used beneath

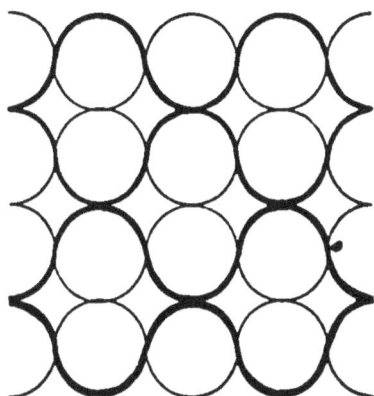

118

119

120

the intersecting-circle pattern. Mr. Mackay considers Figs. 118, 120, and the odd forms on the right in Fig. 130 as derived from the outlines of pottery vessels.[65] Though the forms in Fig. 130 do have some resemblance to certain Harappan vessels, the others in this group do not. It seems more likely that the Fig. 130 forms are detached and degraded members of the contiguous-circle pattern.

[64] *Ibid.*, pl. iii, 7. See also *Arpachiyah*, fig. 66, 5.   [65] *M-d*, p. 328.

Foreign parallels are so rare as to be limited to a single piece. This, appropriately, is found at Tell Halaf itself.[⁴⁴]

There is some probability that the contiguous-circle pattern is a multiplication and outgrowth of the river pattern discussed earlier, since the Tell Halaf specimen is more suggestive of this than of complete circles. Unfortunately, we have no means of checking this possibility. If it be true, it is obvious that it fell under the regularizing influence of the Harappan grid concept.

X

Plant designs. With the Harappan plant motifs we come to a stage of decoration for which there is so little foreign comparable material that we must consider it as a distinctive development, differentiating with finality the painted designs of Harappa from all others. It serves, then, as the first purely local class of decoration with which we have dealt so far. The plant designs appear in such a variety of forms that it is impossible to illustrate them here completely. Only those that appear to be the basic forms, and their most important variations, have been included among the illustrations (Figs. 11, 29, 50, 100, 109, 121-40, 142, 154-7, 173).

It is unnecessary to discuss these plant forms in detail except on occasional points of particular interest. It is also futile to attempt to identify them botanically. Some, no doubt, could be identified if one were thoroughly familiar with the flora of India, but many seem to be an impressionistic representation of vegetation in general. Some are so crowded and confused that one might well imagine that the artist was attempting to show deep jungle rather than specific varieties of trees and plants.[¹⁷]

Fig. 121 illustrates the most clearly defined and least variable of the Harappan plant forms. The leaf is that of the Indian pipal tree (*Ficus religiosa*). As such it never varies markedly from the form shown here, though the stalk from which the leaves sprout seldom has the delicacy characterizing Fig. 121. Because of its use on stamp seals, a phase of Harappan art more widely known than any other, and because of the unvarying outline

⁴⁴ *Tell Halaf*, pl. II, 1.   ¹⁷ See *Sind*, pl. xx, 1, etc.

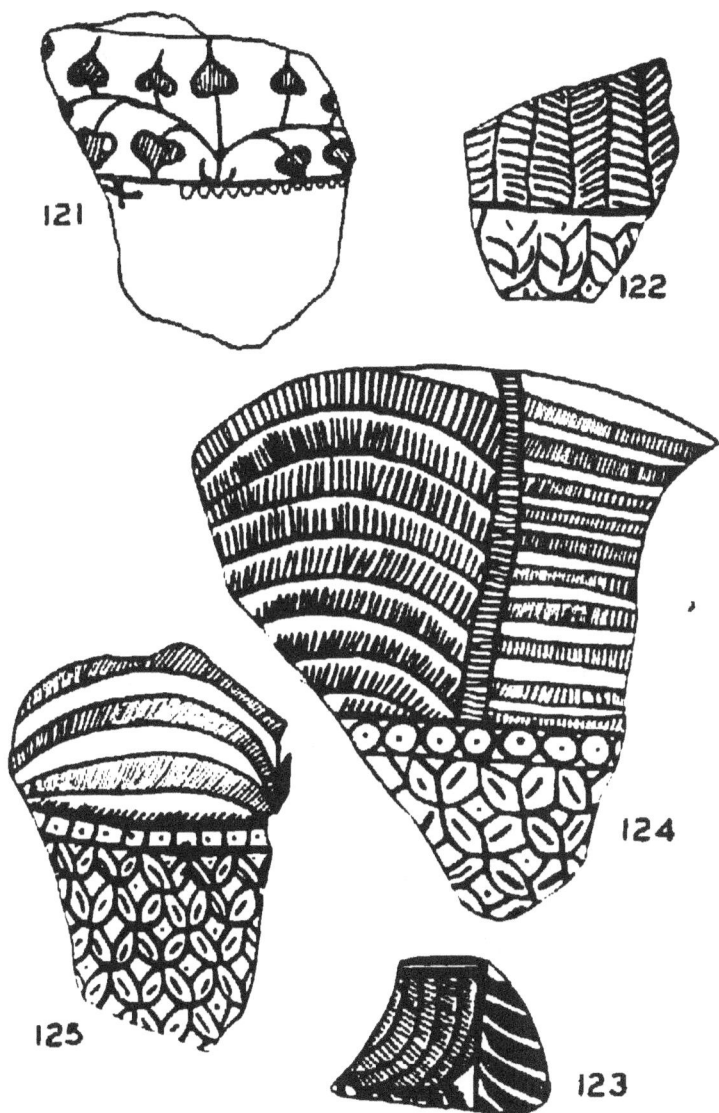

of its leaf, it has come to be known as the most common of all
the Indus plant motifs. Actually it is no more common than
variations of the palm frond type such as are illustrated in Figs.
122-4.

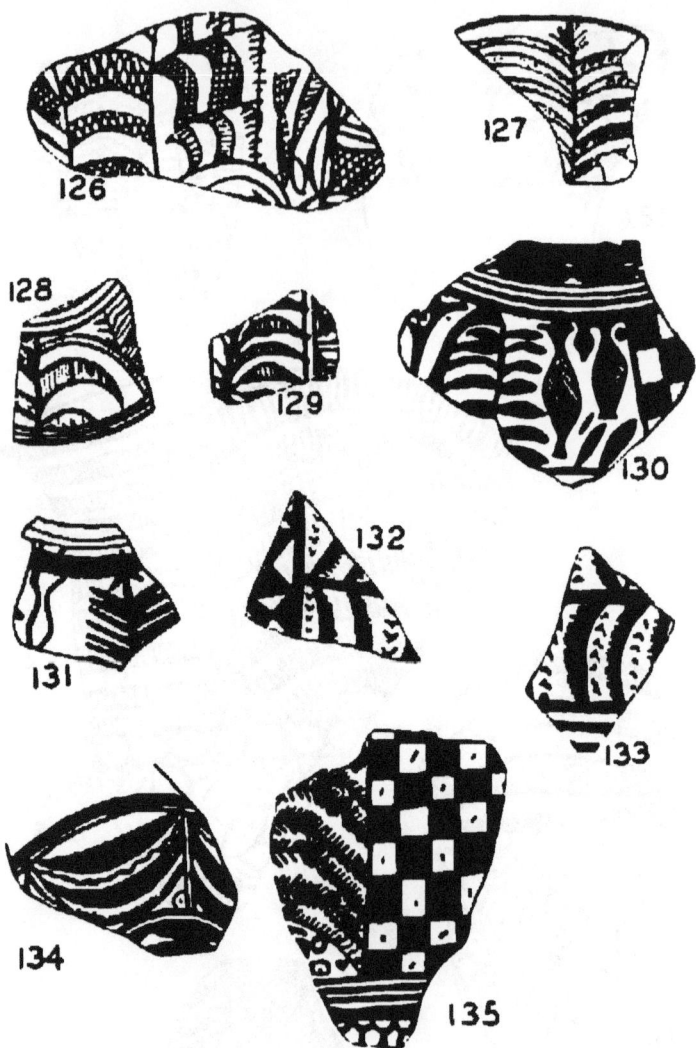

Mackay has called the rows of chevrons seen in Figs. 132 and 133 birds," and from our earlier study of the chevron design this certainly seems to be correct. It will be noted that the type of tree shown here with horizontal trunk is the same which in Fig. 156 grows in the natural upright position.

⁰⁰ *M-d.* p. 328.

136

137

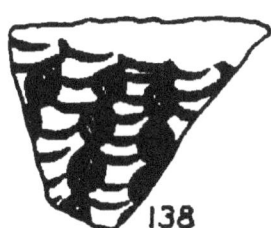

138

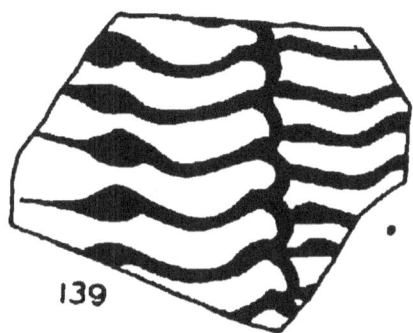

139

140

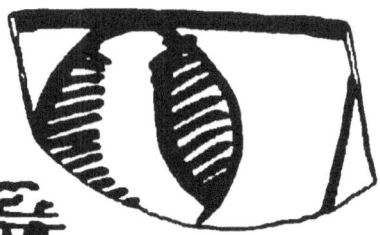

141

The form illustrated in Fig. 138, to which Fig. 139 is related, seems to be taken from aquatic plants, if we may judge from its use in Fig. 173. In fact, if Fig. 173 were to be seen alone, one would be tempted to believe that it represented floats with attached fishhooks, but the many other specimens show clearly that this could not be. This pattern degenerates through stages not shown here to such rudely scrabbled lines as are seen in Fig. 140, giving the impression of dense aquatic or riparian growth.

Attention should be called to the forms seen in Figs. 155 and 157. The large leaves on the right of Fig. 155 apparently grow from an upright trunk just as the two between the animals in Fig. 157 spring from the ground. What is especially interesting is the use of unattached leaves in Fig. 155, a practice encountered repeatedly in Harappan plant scenes.[59] The shape and interior hatching of these leaves is reminiscent of the treatment of the lozenges arising from the intersecting-circle motif, and it is probable that the influence of this familiar geometrical configuration made itself felt in the outline and treatment of similarly shaped leaves. No parallels to this type of design are evident beyond the Indus save in the specimen from Shahi-tump mound illustrated in Fig. 141. The leaf there is still attached to the stalk which is of the frond-like type seen in Fig. 122, etc.

Faint parallels to the frond-like plant (Figs. 122-4) may be cited from Hisar IB-C and Sialk III where single stalks alternate with ibexes or wavy lines.[60] However, it seems unnecessary to derive our Harappan representations from so distant a source when we consider how elemental and logical a form this is for expressing the tropical plants by which the Harappans were surrounded. This and the simple form in which leaves sprout evenly from either side of a central stalk (Fig. 131) are such perfectly natural ways of representing certain basic patterns of plant growth in a simplified way, and are found so consistently throughout Asiatic painted pottery, that we need not consider them as representing more than the vaguest and most remote cultural relationship. In the case of the somewhat more complicated form, in which fringed branches grow on either side of a central trunk, one might wonder about the possibility of a relationship between such Harappan examples as Figs. 132-3,

[59] Cf. fig. 156.
[60] See fig. 152 from Hisar where the edges of the two fronds can be seen before and behind the animal.

156[71] and specimens from the Bampur region in Iran (Fig. 148),[72] or those from Musyan and Khazinah.[73] It is certainly true that there is a greater likeness here than in any of the more elaborate plant forms; but we should not forget that in the plant forms the Harappans were imitating nature. The freedom and realism of all the Harappan specimens show that here they were less bound by tradition than in any other form of design. The potters of Bampur and kindred sites, and to a lesser degree those of Musyan and Khazinah, were also representing what their eyes saw, and it is not to be wondered that all achieved much the same result in depicting the same kind of plant growth.

All in all, there is not one bona fide case of influence or relationship in plant forms between Iran and Mesopotamia on the one hand, and Harappa on the other.[74] Stranger still, the Harappan plant designs as such, with but one exception, do not even penetrate into Baluchistan to the north and west, except as Harappan importations. The exception is the leaf shape seen in Fig. 121, which as the Harappan design *par excellence* travelled along with Harappan power to the neighboring region. This almost complete localization of Harappan plant forms to Harappan sites makes this mode of artistic expression the one true gauge thus far encountered by which we may judge the aesthetic capabilities and impulses of Mohenjo-daro and its related sites. By it we should in the future be able to recognize Harappan influence among objects discovered beyond the basin of the Indus.

XI

Animal designs. Only one representation of humans has been found among the Harappan painted pottery. This is the sherd

[71] See also those on seals: M-d., pls. xii, 16; cxvi, 30.
[72] See also Recems., pl. ix, A. 133; A. 383 + 176. [73] Del. en Perse, viii, figs. 192-5.
[74] The possible relationship between figs. 155 and 141, cited above, is not really a valid *foreign* parallel since we have previously noted the cultural relationships between Shahi-tump and Harappa through Kulli, Mehi, and Amri.
  One might at first sight see a relationship between the crudely knobbed branches of M-d., 1937-31, pl. lxviii, 8 and such earlier western examples as Samarra, pl. xvi, or Sialk, pl. lxxxiii, B, 1. However, the resemblance on the part of Harappa is so faint, and the careless confusion of its rendering so in keeping with the spirit of other Harappan plant scenes, that the likeness is in all probability fortuitous.

142

143

144

from Harappa itself illustrated in Fig. 142.[91] One will note at
once the naturalism and sound proportions that set these apart
from all other prehistoric human figures. Even the fragmentary
Amri man, Fig. 143, has infinitely more of the primitive about
it than these. In spite of the accomplished manner in which the
Harappan figures are shown, the hands are depicted upraised,
perhaps in adoration, exactly as they are in the Susian pottery
and with a very much earlier painted pottery human, Fig. 144,
from Persepolis. One might compare our Harappan example
with the graceful line of figures from Khazinah,[90] for there is
a resemblance between the two. But when we consider the
amazingly accomplished sculpture from Harappa, it seems unnecessary to go all the way to Elam to explain the grace of the
people in Fig. 142. In view of the conservatism of the Harappan
painted pottery as a whole, it is curious that here conservatism
should have been abandoned. In the Harappan sculpture, relief
and in the round, we see two distinct schools. One is represented
by the votive figurines in which naturalism has been foresworn
in favor of the conventional and ancient patterns dictated by

[91] The ankles and feet of both figures are unclear in the original illustration, but there
is a suggestion, with the larger figure, of feet shown in profile, both pointing to the right.
[90] Dél. en Perse, VIII, fig. 254.

[70]

cult usage. The other school—which produced the statues and seals—shows with startling accuracy the scene or figure as the artist saw it. In Fig. 142 the artist appears to have been a follower of the latter school.

The lower animals on Harappan pottery appear to be largely dominated by forms and artistic conventions peculiar to the west. This manifests itself either in grouping, species, or details of rendering. The crowded lines of tiny animals seen in Harappan Figs. 145 and 146 have close parallels in the specimens from Bampur, Figs. 147 and 148. The Harappan stags in Fig. 149

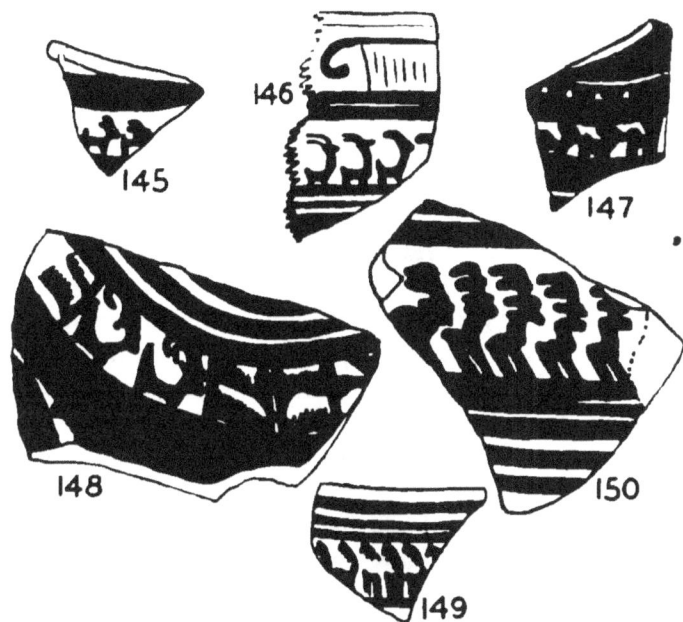

show this same crowded grouping, and the similarly cramped example from Amri, Fig. 150, has almost exact parallels in Bampur.[97] Such regimented arrangement is quite different from the animal scenes which through their associated plant forms may be considered as more characteristically Harappan, and they lack entirely the freedom that one sees among the plant patterns.

[97] *Reconn.*, pl. vii.

Incidentally, the doe in Fig. 142 seems to be less restrained by foreign conventions than any of the other Harappan quadrupeds. Returning to these compact rows of little animals, it is quite certain that they stem from the older tradition of Iran and Mesopotamia. In Halaf levels, quadrupeds and birds are so arranged, and in Susa I tight rows of small birds are common as borders. In Gawra XIII (al-'Ubaid period) we again see small quadrupeds in close file,[98] and among the very early wares of Fars we find birds and animals so treated at Tal-i-skau and Tal-i-regi (Khusu).[99] In Hisar I and Sialk III we have not only birds and humans but also a similar grouping of ibexes and tigers, while at Musyan and Khazinah we see this regimentation at its height. The Harappan stags (Fig. 149), particularly, have parallels with Musyan and Khazinah, not only in respect to the details of the head but in the accentuation of the toothed antlers as well.[100]

One need not assume that with the rams and ibexes the Harappans were depicting animals with which they were wholly unacquainted. There is good reason to believe that they were familiar with both. Bones of sheep have been found among the ruins at Mohenjo-daro, and the presence of ibex within fifty miles of the region today[101] supports the impression of naturalism one feels in the Harappan example, Fig. 151. It is the grouping that springs from the west. With the stags one cannot be so sure that the grouping alone is the foreign element. It is true that four different types of deer horns have been recovered from Mohenjo-daro, but only one of these, that of the Kashmir Stag (*Cervus cashmerianus*), has sufficiently pronged antlers to have been the inspiration for Fig. 149. Moreover, only two examples were found—against eighteen, one, and six specimens of each of the other three varieties. The fact that only antlers, and no bones, were unearthed has led Messrs. Sewell and Guha to suggest that all were imported as such.[102] It does not seem likely, judging from the present habitat, that all the species were foreign importations, but the present upland home of the Kashmir Stag suggests that it at least could

[98] *Bull. A.S.O.R.*, no. 66, fig. 7.
[100] *Del. en Perse*, VIII, figs. 212-9.
[102] *Ibid.*, pp. 671-2.

[99] *Perse*, pls. xxiv, 10; xxv, 11, 15.
[101] *M-d*, p. 322.

not have been entirely familiar to the Harappans. Looking at the painted form, one can see how far it is from nature; certainly much more so than would have been the case had the artist been drawing an animal familiar to him in real life. This aspect lends strength to the connection implied earlier between our example and those of the type seen at Musyan and Khazinah. Turning now to our other representation of an animal with many-tined antlers, Fig. 155, we can see how wholly unrealistic it is.[103] It is obvious that the artist was drawing a beast he had heard of but never seen. In fact, the resemblance in horn treatment to one from Susa I[104] is so close that we may feel certain that here the Harappan artist was reproducing a traditional form, entirely without regard for nature. Had he been familiar with the animal, such horn treatment would have been absurd. Thus we see that not only in grouping were the Harappans following the custom of the west but, at least in this case, in the kind of animal to be represented as well.

Another widespread convention having parallels in the earlier pottery of the west is illustrated by the marks above and below

the animals in Fig. 151. That the introduction of a separate decorative motif, particularly over the back, originally had some well-understood significance is shown by the way it has persisted from early times into this late period. Nor does it have the aspect of spacefilling in the earlier examples, though if one were to see Fig. 151 alone such an assumption would be justified.[105] In Fig.

[103] See also M-d, 1927-31, pl. lxx, 29. That the markings here represent tines and not simply corrugations is shown by their presence only on one side of the beams. Corrugated horns are sometimes indicated on the seals by markings on both sides (cf. M-d, pl. ciii, 11, 16; etc.).

[104] Dél. en Perse, xiii, pl. xvi, 1.

[105] That the lines below the necks in fig. 151 do not represent a beard (cf. fig. 152) seems certain from the complete absence of this feature on other Harappan animals.

152, for example, the animal from Hisar IC has below it a row of small horizontal lines (almost dots) while above, within the curl of the horns, is a six-armed cross. Much the same symbol appears above the backs of the Halaf animals (a circle surrounded by dots), while in Susa I, we see within the curve of the horns, or over the back, various elaborate symbols the meanings of which are lost; others show detached horns with a circle-and-dot symbol identical with the Halaf specimens.[104] In Sialk III, various crosses and "suns" are used, while at Persepolis a peculiar grating-like figure appears over the back as shown in Figs. 167 and 153.[107] Only Samarra and Musyan fail to use some such convention.[108] The introduction of a decoration below the body is less common but equally early. From Persepolis we see both above and below the lion-like animal in Fig. 153 a rectangular grid which is but a repetition of the inner field of the symbols seen in the Persepolitan example, Fig. 167. Along with these are potent crosses and what

153   154

seem to be sprigs of vegetation. The latter have distant parallels in the leaf patterns below the Harappan animals of Figs. 154-6. The former may be equated with the crosses of Hisar I and Sialk III and, as outlined earlier, with the sun-like symbol over the back of the animal in Fig. 142. Decoration below the body appears also in Giyan V, Hisar IB and IC, and Sialk III.[109] Among the Harappan examples, Fig. 154 has a leaf-shaped figure beneath the belly of

[104] Del. en Perse, xiii, pl. v, 3.
[107] This can certainly be equated with the checkered symbols of Susa I.
[108] Al-'Ubaid is practically devoid of animal figures.
[109] Giyan, pls. 57, 59; Hisar, pls. v, vii, x-xiii; Sialk, pl. lxxxi, etc.

the animal, while below the neck is a snake. In Fig. 155 we see the leaf-like patterns above and below the upper animal, that below perhaps being another snake. Again the connected leaf motif is repeated over the back of the lower beast. In Fig. 156 the leaf-shaped and circular figures are not only above and below the animal but behind it as well. This disposition is seen also in our examples from Persepolis, Figs. 153 and 167. Most convincing

155

156

of all is the symbol above the back of the animal in Fig. 142. In the discussion of the comb motif this figure was identified, provisionally, as a sun symbol, and it was equated with the six-armed pommée cross of Hisar (Fig. 152) and the dotted circle of Halaf and Susa I. These foreign symbols appear in exactly the same relation to the animal, or its horns, as the rayed circle of Fig. 142.

Fig. 156 illustrates another Harappan peculiarity reminiscent of a common western convention—a smaller animal on the back of a larger one. It is possible that all the artist was attempting was to show an attack by this jackal-like animal on the buffalo,[110] but scenes in which action or struggle may be implied are so strikingly

110 Mackay considers figs. 156 and 151 as possible importations because of the thinness of the ware (M-d, p. 324).

[75]

absent in all other Harappan painted sherds that it seems unlikely here. Our earliest comparable design comes from Persepolis where we have a large-horned beast with above it a dog-like animal in exactly the same relationship as seen here.[111] Related to Persepolis in culture, and presumably close to it in time, is Tal-i-siah (Madavan) in Fars where we see smaller animals both above and behind ibexes.[112] In Sialk III we have tigers attacking ibexes, and in Levels II and III the more common usage of birds above the backs of larger horned beasts.[113] In Susa I, we have both small quadrupeds

and flying birds shown over the backs of ibexes,[114] and in Giyan V we see birds, both flying and at rest, above similarly horned animals.[115] If there is any doubt about the relationship of this convention to Fig. 156, there can be none with Fig. 142 where two birds are shown, one flying above the animal and one perched on its back.

[111] Appearing in Dr. Herzfeld's forthcoming book (Oxford University Press) on Iranian archaeology.

[112] Perse, pl. xiii, 44, 46.

[113] Sialk, pls. xlix, A, 15; lxxiii, C, 3, 4, 6. Birds so placed become a very common motif on the cylinder seals of early Sumerian times.

[114] Del. en Perse, xiii, pl. iii, 5; Persian Art, iv, pl. 5, C   [115] Giyan, pls. 47, 54

Another peculiarity that many of the Harappan animals share with the west is the practice of depicting the bodies by hatching or crosshatching within heavy bordering lines. For Harappa this is illustrated by Figs. 151, 154-9, 168, and 173. In Iran proper we see it used in Sialk II (Figs. 86-7), and Sialk III satisfies the convention by the use of dots in depicting tigers and hatching for the snakes.[110] Basically the same convention of hatching is found in the sherd from the post-Persepolitan site Tal-i-regi (Khusu), Fig. 160, and in Hisar IC (dots) and IIA.[111] At Samarra the principle is adhered to in the triangle pattern on the bodies of the stags, while in the Halaf culture we have both the usual diagonal hatching, and a closely dotted interior within a heavy outline.[112] Finally, in Susa II (Fig. 161) we see it as fully established in Elam as it was at Mohenjo-daro. Why certain of the Harappan animals were so shown, while others were not, is largely a matter of size, such a practice being impossible with figures as small as those of Figs. 145 and 149. However, the solid coloring of the doe in Fig 142 from Harappa itself cannot be laid to size. The

162

naturalism of the human figures on this sherd has already been pointed out, and it is just as obvious that the doe is free of those distortions and conventionalizations that mark the other quadrupeds. It is, in fact, close to the style of the seals, which will be discussed later as wholly Indian, in contradistinction to the bulk of painted designs whose domination by the west is clear. We may

[110] *Sialk*, pls. lxii, S. 1693; lxvii, S. 152.
[111] *Hisar*, pls. vii, H 4502, etc.; xxi, H 4460. Stylized tigers with hatched bodies, like the Hisar example in *Samarra*, pl. xliv, q², are found at Persepolis.
[112] *Arpachiyah*, fig. 77, 1, *Halaf*, pl. liii, 10.

assume, then, that this specimen represents the rare and truly Indian form of animal representation.

The final peculiarity of Harappan animal representation is the graphic way in which the eye is shown (Figs. 145, 156, 159, 168-9). Even the Amri ibex, Fig. 162, shows an attempt at this same wide-eyed aspect. The only markedly earlier precedents for this practice in lands beyond the Indus and Baluchistan are in the snake figures

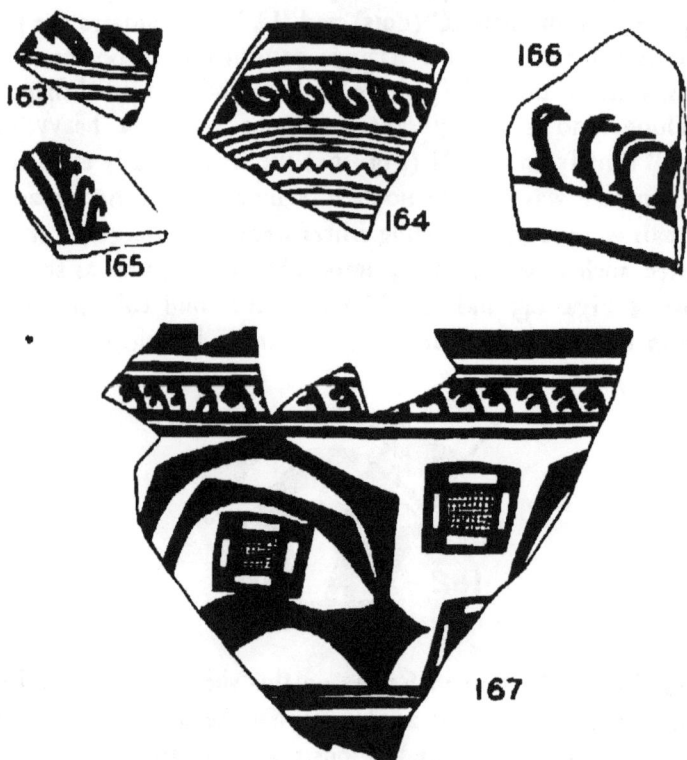

from Susa I, illustrated in Fig. 172, B, C, at Musyan and Khazinah, and in levels of Halaf culture in Mesopotamia.[114] It is probable that the Harappa-like eye treatment of the Susa II animal, Fig. 161, is an indirect descendant of the Susa I convention.

[114] *Del. en Perse*, VIII, figs. 198, 239-40; *Halaf*, pl. liii, 6, 9, 10, 14, 15; *Bull. A.S.O.R.*, 65, p. 7, fig. 4.

Intimately related to the horned animals just discussed is the symbol for the ibex or bighorn sheep which among the Harappan designs appears in the form illustrated by Fig. 163. The Amri design of Fig. 164 seems quite certainly to be the same thing, though the direction has become reversed. Another Harappan example, presumably belonging to this class, is seen in Fig. 165,[119] which may be taken as a simplification of a more pictorial form such as that from Baluchistan seen in Fig. 166. Ample precedent for such symbolization exists in the west. At Persepolis we see it in the border of the sherd illustrated in Fig. 167, and again at the Persepolitan site Tal-i-pir in southern Fars.[120] In the Halaf culture we have a great multitude of bucrania,[121] which though different in detail represent the same concept of symbolizing an animal by depicting only its most prominent visual feature. At Musyan and Khazinah the bucranium is also found, though because of a certain similarity it is sometimes erroneously thought of as a human with upraised arms.[122] In Susa I we have the curved lines

which we have already identified as horns through their association with the dotted circle.[123] And at the same site the animal is again symbolized, or abbreviated, by the horns alone in one case and by the head and horns in another.[124] Closer to the Indus even than Persepolis, we find it in an antler-like style as a common motif on the Khurab pottery.[125]

Birds on the Harappan pottery, in their symbolized form, have already been studied in some detail under the discussion of the

[119] For an identical Amri example see *Sind*, pl. xxiv, 34.
[120] *Recomm.*, pl. xxix, iv. 16; iv. 21-2: iv. 25; v. 46.
[121] *Arpachiyah*, figs. 74, 75, 76, etc.   [122] *Del. en Perse*, viii, figs. 306, 255-60.
[123] *Ibid.*, xiii, pl. v, 3. See also pl. vi, 1; pl. vii, 2, 7; pl. ix, 2.
[124] *Ibid.*, figs. 2, 135.   [125] *Recomm..* pl. xvi, B. ii. 132, 136, 137, 147, etc.

chevron design. However, naturalistic representations also exist. Here the Harappan bird *par excellence* is the peafowl (Figs. 168, 142 far right). It is not only the commonest bird, but it appears more often than all the other animal forms combined; and it is not found further afield than central Baluchistan, within the Harappan sphere of influence. The form that this creature takes is so completely naturalistic and so devoid of the distortions of misunderstood convention that we must consider it as entirely Indian in inspiration. Only the hatched bodies suggest western influence. The only other type of naturalistic bird—a jungle fowl of some sort—is far less common. Fig. 169 is the most graphic example. It, too, appears to be a drawing from life rather than a rendition of a traditional form. It is seen again in the bird at rest in the left-hand panel of Fig. 142, while the bird in flight—on the

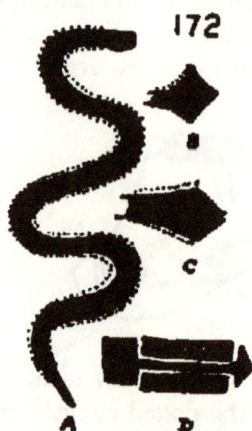

same sherd—is identical in outline with pottery bird figurines from Mohenjo-daro.[120] This is one of those rare instances in which a painted design shows any marked resemblances to Harappan figures in other media, another instance being the doe on this same remarkable sherd.

Snakes frequently appear among the pottery designs and occasionally on the seals. Fig. 170 shows the snake used alone, while in Figs. 154 and 155 D they appear below ibexes. In Fig. 134 what

120 M-d, pl. xcvi, 1.

may be a snake is shown among the dense plants making up the
pattern. At Amri snakes are shown in greater detail though with
no greater naturalism (Fig. 171). It is impossible to present valid
related parallels to such elemental figures. Any primitive or un-
skilled person would be apt to show a snake as the Harappans
did in Fig. 170, without any other model than the mental image
of the snake itself. Suffice it to say that it has none of the refine-
ments or conventions of the Halaf serpent[127] or of the Susian types
shown in Fig. 172, A-C. And it is even further removed from the
Susa I snake symbol of Fig. 172, D, and similar motifs from
Persepolis.[128]

The final animal figures to come under consideration are the
fishes shown in Fig. 173. Both appear to be caught on lines extending from the bulbous figures discussed under *Plant designs*. No

173

ancient Asiatic parallels to these exist to my knowledge, other
than the late figures from Nal[129] and the roughly contemporary
fishes from Susa II.[130]

In looking over the evidence presented by the animal figures,
one sees that the relationship with the west, which was almost
wholly lacking with the plant designs, is strongly manifest here.
Nor is this surprising, in view of the important rôle played by
animals, or conventions derived from animals, in the early pottery
of Iran, Elam, and Mesopotamia. The recognizable western tradi-

[127] *Arpachiyah*, fig. 77, 9.
[128] *Persepolis*, pl. xxvii, top row center. The more complete specimens are appearing
in Dr. Herzfeld's forthcoming book on Iranian archaeology.
[129] *Nal*, pl. 21, b.   [130] *Del. en Perse*, xiii, ph. xxv, xxxi.

[81]

tions are seen first in the rows of squat, closely crowded animals. Second is the use of animals (stags) which there is reason to believe were unfamiliar to the Harappans in real life. In fact, the grotesque appearance of such beasts as are shown in Figs. 154-7 would suggest that here, too, the artists were not drawing from real life but were reproducing as best they could traditional forms of much earlier origin. Certainly they do not compare in skill or realism with the figures on Fig. 142, or the peafowl, or the plants. The third sign of western convention is seen in various details of rendering, such as the use of symbols, animals and marks above and below the main figure, hatched or crosshatched bodies, accentuation of the eye, and the use of horns alone to symbolize a whole animal.

Again, but unlike the plant designs, many of the conventions by which the animals of Harappan pottery are rendered appear also in the major sites of Baluchistan. We have already noted the similarity between the fishes of Chanhu-daro (Fig. 173) and those of Nal. Similarly, a comparison of the animal forms of Kulli, Mehi, and Periano-ghundai, to take but a few, will show crosshatched bodies, the same eye treatment, and the same disposition of objects above and below the body as in Harappa. In this we have the first link in the chain of western parallels.

No attempt has been made here to classify the animals as to species. Such terms as "ibex" or "mountain goat" are used only in their most general meaning.

XII

Miscellaneous. The pattern shown in Fig. 174 has no parallels from non-Harappan sites, nor does it appear very often on painted pottery within its own culture. However, the outline as such was perfectly familiar to the Harappans, for we see it in shell and faïence as inlay,[131] and as applied and engraved decoration on imitation carnelian and on silver.[132] Mr. Mackay pointed in the right direction when he suggested a comparison of this form with the "trappings (?) on the withers of the so-called unicorn"

131 *M-d*, pl. clv, 38-47.   132 *Ibid.*, pls. clvi, 13; clvii, 10, 11.

174

of the seals.[111] It will be seen that this beast is almost invariably
represented with a kind of ceremonial saddlecloth over the back,
the one visible end of which is heart-shaped in the manner of our
pottery representation. That this actually is a caparison and not
an imaginative representation of skin folds or muscle ridges is
shown by distinct tassels on one example, and on another by an
indented border which breaks up the outline into separate contiguous areas just as in Fig. 174.[112] Also of interest is the double
outline on all the seal examples, agreeing with the inner and outer
borders of those in Fig. 174. That the two forms of representation
are really one and the same is shown by two copper plates from
Mohenjo-daro, on which animal figures are engraved.[113] Apparently from inadeptness, which is obvious from the composition
as a whole, the craftsman here has placed on the flank of each
animal not the ceremonial trapping seen in the seals but a simple
figure identical in outline with the outer borders of those in
Fig. 174. Whether the simple Fig. 174 form is an imitation of the
essentials of the ceremonial saddlecloth, or the other way around,
is uncertain, but the latter would seem more likely, for it will be
noted that the engraver of the copper examples placed the heart-
shaped figures with the cleft up, which would not have been
appropriate had he been imitating the edge of the cloth rather
than the form from which this edge was patterned.

No true foreign parallels to this design exist, but an interesting
related form is found in an Elamite cylinder seal of the Jumdat

[111] Ibid., p. 568.
[113] Ibid., pls. cxvii, 7; cxviii, 3.
[112] Ibid., pls. ciii, 18; civ, 34.

Nasr period.[136] Here we see a bull charging a lion—a bull with a saddlecloth which differs from the Harappan form only in having a straight rather than a scalloped lower border.[137] This unexpected appurtenance, as well as the exaggerated rendering of skin folds, the stippling to show the skin texture, and the marked lance-shaped tuft on the end of the tail, all combine to show that this creature was directly inspired by a Harappan seal representation. The scattered plants above and below the beast—a feature never seen in the Harappan seals—may hark back to the painted pottery technique observed in Figs. 154-7. The particular importance of these likenesses lies in their demonstration of the currency of developed Harappan designs and technique in Elam as early as the time of Jumdat Nasr.[138]

One peculiar and distinctive pattern that may be included here is found, so far as I know, only in the very deep strata of Mohenjo-daro and in Level 2b of Nineveh. The latter is equated with the Halaf period. The pattern is of the all-over variety, and consists of parallel horizontal lines continuously connected by closely set, roughly parallel, wavy lines. This unusual correspondence of design between two such distant sites again brings into prominence the points of similarity between the pottery of the Halaf culture and that of the Indus Valley.[139]

[136] See particularly H. Frankfort, *Cylinder Seals* (London, 1939), pl. vii, a; also *Del. en Perse*, xvi, figs. 93, 161.

[137] Cf. *M-d*, pl. cx, 321.

[138] Another Harappan feature observable in Elamite seals of Jumdat Nasr date is the characteristic step-pyramid design: cf. *Del. en Perse*, xii, pl. i, 137, and xvi, pl. xvii, 263 with *M-d*, pl. clv, 31-5. It is also possible that the exclusively Indian plant, the pipal, was the inspiration for such leaf forms as seen in *Del. en Perse*, xvi, fig. 139.

[139] Unfortunately, these examples came to my attention too late to be included among the illustrations of this volume. See, however, *M-d, 1927-31*, pl. xcii, 7 and *Liv. Annals*, xx, pl. xxxviii, 17.

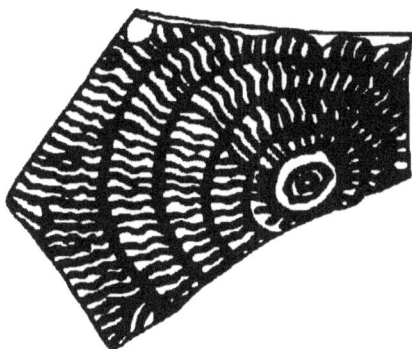

PART III

CONCLUSIONS

I

IN summing up the material cited above, one cannot but be struck by the large number of motifs that are common both to Harappa and the prehistoric world west of the Indus. Certain of these designs, to be sure, might and apparently have occurred to separated and unrelated peoples quite independently. In this class should be put the single or multiple parallel lines separating vases into registers or panels, the looped line, the checker pattern, and the rows of connected lozenges. However, rows of lozenges used as an all-over pattern are restricted to Sialk II (one example), and to Halaf culture levels, where it is a common repeat pattern. One would expect to find the fish-scale pattern developing naturally everywhere that the loop was used, but actually it appears only in the Halaf culture, Sialk III, Giyan V, Tal-i-regi (Khusu), and Tal-i-skau, the last two sites yielding sherds of a developed Persepolis style.

The loop-man motif, in one variation or another, appears in a variety of sites and cultures extending from Amri, through Kalat-i-gird in the Helmand Delta, Tal-i-skau and Tal-i-Sang-i-siah in Fars, Hisar IB, Sialk I-III, and Samarra, while its most naturalistic form is seen in Halaf sites.

[85]

The river pattern cannot very well be considered a fortuitous discovery by unrelated peoples, yet it is found almost universally, in one form or another, from the Indus to the upper reaches of the Euphrates.

The use of sigmas and chevrons, representing birds in flight, is another almost universal convention among our prehistoric cultures. Its most realistic versions come from Samarra, but the main theatre of use is Elam and the southern half of Iran.

The "comb animal" is far more limited in its spread. Its most active patrons were the potters of Susa I, while Giyan IV introduces its most florid phase. If the comb originated in the manner illustrated by Sialk II usage, we may consider it to be a Central Iranian concept.

The "sun" symbol seen with the Harappan combs appears repeatedly in Sialk III, and it is clearly related to the dotted circle of Halaf and Susa I and to the concentric circles of Susa II. It is as closely related to the Hisar dot-circle and dotted circle which, by being interchangeable with the pommée cross, relates also to the form seen at Persepolis (Fig. 153) and the plain six- and eight-armed crosses seen consistently in Fars and Kirman.

Among the grid patterns, single and uncertain examples of the opposed-triangle design (Fig. 96) occur at Samarra and Musyan, one true specimen from Tal-i-skau in Fars, and considerable numbers in Sialk III and at Halaf sites. The intersecting-circle pattern, with its variations, appears in the west only in Halaf culture levels. The same is true of the contiguous-circle pattern.

The Harappan plant designs show no significant likeness to those of the west.

With the animal figures, closely crowded rows of small animals are found in Halaf levels, Gawra XIII (al-'Ubaid period), Susa I, Tal-i-skau and Tal-i-regi (Khusu) in Fars, Sialk II-III, and Hisar I. Musyan and Khazinah present the most active use of this convention; while the closest likeness to our Harappan specimens are in examples from the sites on the Bampur river in Kirman. The convention of showing above or below the larger quadrupeds a symbol or animal is found at Persepolis, Halaf, Susa I, Tal-i-siah

[86]

(Madavan) in Fars, Hisar IB and IC, Sialk III, and Giyan V. The convention of showing the body by hatching or other open patterns within broad borders is found at Samarra, Halaf, Persepolis, Tal-i-regi (Khusu), Hisar IC (dots) and IIA, Sialk II-III, and Susa II. Accentuation of the eye is found in Susa I and II, at Musyan and Khazinah, which like Susa are within the boundaries of Elam, and in the Halaf levels of Tell Halaf and Tepe Gawra in Mesopotamia. Detached horns as a symbol for the animal are found at Persepolis and its contemporary Tal-i-pir, Halaf, Susa I, and the Khurab burials.

From this very brief summary one can see not only how many motifs and patterns found at Harappan sites appear also in the west but over how large an area this western field extends and how uniformly most of these patterns are represented in this area.[1] Since we have no closely comparable ware from India or Baluchistan that is clearly and demonstrably older than Harappan, it becomes certain that the elements shared by Harappa with the west are an inheritance from the more ancient cultures of Iran, Elam, and Mesopotamia. In fact, except for the plant motifs, a few of the animals, and the queer form illustrated in Fig. 174, there is not a single decorative element, not one pattern or motif, that does not have a correspondent among the earlier cultures of the west.

It is very doubtful whether such a hold could be had through borrowing alone. In this respect one should not overlook the evidence offered by the remarkably unmixed nature of Harappan objects as a whole. One of the most notable peculiarities of Harappan sites is the almost complete absence of objects that may be positively identified as contemporary importations. We know, for instance, that there was considerable Indian contact with Sumer, for numbers of Harappan seals and beads have been

[1] It is natural that each decorative unit is not represented at each site examined, for we must allow for differences in culture, for regional differences in style, and for differences in time. Also, many of the sites with which we have had to deal have been but scantily excavated. A large number of correspondents have been noted among the finds of Susa I. Important though this is, one should remember that Susa has been very extensively excavated, and it is only natural that it would present more correspondents to foreign motifs than can be found in the smaller excavations.

found in that land. Yet the contact would seem to have been almost wholly one-sided, for not even that most-often-lost of objects, the Sumerian or Babylonian cylinder seal, is found in India.[1] Nor is there more than the most meager evidence in Harappa of other objects and practices of foreign origination, save for those of such elemental nature as can be explained by common descent from much more remote times. This remarkable, and at present inexplicable, isolation is a powerful argument against the possibility of the acquisition of such a repertoire of foreign decorative motifs by the Harappans through borrowing alone, since they are demonstrably so unreceptive to foreign innovations in their other arts and crafts. We may also assume that the features that Harappan painted designs share with such late wares as Susa II and Jumdat Nasr (prominent eye, hatched bodies, etc.) do not necessarily represent an interchange of ideas—west to east, at least—so much as they do the logical and inevitable evolution from earlier prototypes.

Side by side with this western-engendered series is a smaller group of decorated pottery, headed by the plant designs, which appear as a distinct local or Indian development. Of these there will be more to say later.

One cannot but be struck by the labored and decadent appearance of the occidentally dominated designs. The heaviness of line seen in all but a few, the lack of originality, and the general tired look gives the impression of an art long established and slavishly copied. In addition to this, we have the fact that the excavators of Mohenjo-daro were unable to detect any significant stylistic change between the earliest and the latest painted pieces from that site, though there is a noticeable decrease in the number of specimens in the later levels. The general lack of any marked regional differences in style between the various Harappan sites adds to the impression of standardization. Even the plant designs, which seem to be India's main contribution among the decorative elements, tend to fall into well-defined categories as though their forms, too, were gradually becoming inviolate.

[1] Three cylinder seals have been found at Mohenjo-daro (M-d, 1927-31, nos. 78, 376, 488), but none can be considered as anything other than Indian in workmanship.

All this, in conjunction with the heaviness of the ware so decorated—in contrast to the delicate fabrics of earlier times in the west—points to a conscious retention of a much earlier decorative style faithfully repeated from generation to generation. With this we have the relative rarity of painted specimens at Harappan sites to show this as a custom kept alive not by the desire for natural artistic expression but by the demands of some custom. In this respect the simpler, everyday Harappan ware is of interest. We see that far from being plain it is oftener than not decorated with horizontal bands of black pigment, often on the same types of vessels that under other circumstances were elaborately decorated. These simple bands seem to be the last vestiges of a more universal decoration which for some special reason was retained only on occasional pieces. The motivating force behind the retention of the more elaborate decoration cannot be discerned, but it is most probable that it was in some way religious. There is good reason for believing that the patterns on the earlier wares of Iran and Mesopotamia originated as primitive magical—hence religious—symbols or pictures. Consequently, it is quite possible that some understanding of the early significance of the designs was inherited as well. If this is correct, we must assume that the primitive cult so observed was quite distinct from that served or illumined by the seals and the sculpture, for they are radically different in subject and feeling from these painted designs.

While the Harappans were obeying the dictates of a tradition essentially foreign to the Indus, they were at the same time expressing themselves in the seals, the sculpture, and in certain of the painted pottery designs—namely, the plant patterns and such rare animal forms as those illustrated in Figs. 142, 168, and 169—in a manner entirely different in feeling. There is a certain freedom and spontaneity about this group that suggests a culturally advanced people expressing themselves in a natural fashion. Since we have no other ancient fields of Asiatic art in any way comparable to this, we are justified in assuming it to be a local form of expression uninhibited by foreign artistic conventions. Thus we have marked for us with extraordinary clarity the two groups of Harappan artistic expression: one fathered by western Asia, the other by the Indus.

II

Sir John Marshall has based his classification of the Harappan and Baluchi painted pottery mainly upon the color of the background, calling that with the red-slip background characteristically East Baluchi and Indian, and that with the light background characteristically western.' It should be remembered, however, that Harappan painted pottery is not uniformly red slipped, but may be light red, pink, cream, or buff. Even the gray ware is painted, but only with horizontal bands around the body of the vessel. Thus we see that what is taken as the hallmark for Harappan painted ware characterizes the majority and not the whole. It would seem to mark a preference rather than the demand of a hard and fast tradition. Since the time when Marshall wrote, the ware of Amri has been discovered which is wholly buff' and which is as widely spread along the Indus (so far as it has been systematically explored) as Harappan ware. Here we see the red slip ceasing to be the insignia for Indian ware as a whole and narrowed down to Harappan in general.

Turning westward, to the supposed stronghold of the buff wares, we find in Anau I the use of a "very thin, fine, light-brown or light reddish-brown color slip," while in Anau II the slip becomes "generally light-red in firing . . . Brown vessels also occurred"; even Anau IV used the red slip.' It should be added that the lack of uniformity in ground color of the earlier Anau specimens gives the impression that the outcome—buff, red, or brown—was unpremeditated and accidental. In Hisar IA-B the decoration is painted on a "brown-red ground," while in IIA "red or brown vessels, often with flaked-off slip" are reported.' Sialk I, II, and III also manufactured wares with a red ground color. Musyan and late Susa I both produced red-slip ware, attributed by Frankfort, in the case of Susa, to northern influence.' In Gawra XII the slip

' M-I. pp. 97-101.
' A very few exceptions are found: fig. 171 is black paint on a red ground.
' Turkestan, pp. 131 (pls. 22-3), 133, 146.   ' Hisar. p. 40.
' Studies, pp. 38-9. Del. en Perse, VIII, p. 92; XX, p. 100.

is "... almost exclusively red, deep and glossy ...,"[7] while the pottery of the Uruk period is characterized by its red slip, a tradition which is thought to have come from Anatolia, the traditional home of burnished red-slip ware. Moreover, the earliest ware found at Tell Halaf is a burnished red intermixed with sherds of black and gray.[8] And finally, Mackay says, "The brilliance of the slips on some of the Jemdet Nasr pottery is only equalled by that of the red ware of predynastic Egypt and of the painted pottery of Mohenjo-Daro."[10]

Thus we see that what Marshall considers as the basic characteristic of western pottery really only demarks the custom or preference of certain districts or groups of people. By the same tokens, red or buff ground ceases to be the guide by which eastern and western wares may be differentiated. Consequently, the typical red slip of Harappa does not set that pottery apart as unmistakably eastern, or Indian, or Harappan. It merely denotes a regional or group preference shared at random by east and west alike. There is, then, no real incongruity in the presence of western designs on the so-called "Indian" red-slip background of Harappa.

III

With all the likeness in detail and ground color between Harappa and the west, one is confronted by the paradox that as a whole the Harappan painted ware gives none of the impression of Iranian or Mesopotamian painted pottery. It has an appearance that is wholly individual. Though western decorative elements were inherited, they were rendered in a way that was not just eastern or Indian, but Harappan. This air of individuality is apparent on even the most casual inspection of the designs as a whole. To take but a single example, compare the river pattern of Figs. 29 and 136 with the multitudinous examples from Iran and Mesopotamia. The differences in rendition and feeling are at once obvious. Only in the most elemental patterns, such as

[8] *Bull. A.S.O.R.*, no. 68 (Dec., 1937), p. 9.
[9] *Halaf*, p. 208; see also Nineveh 1 in *Nineveh, 1931-3*, p. 151.
[10] *Jemdet Nasr*, p. 245. Later than the bulk of Jumdat Nasr, but pertinent here, is the so-called "scarlet ware" of Middle Babylonia.

the simple wavy line or the lozenges, in which there is little chance for individual expression, is the likeness reasonably close. Idiosyncrasies of style also set the animals apart from all others, though they fall into the same broad stylistic pattern as those of eastern Baluchistan.

When we say that the painted pottery is individually Harappan it must be understood that the individuality does not imply an artistic unity with Harappan objects in other media, but only applies to the painted pottery of western inspiration as a distinct and unmistakable unit. This brings us to the second paradox, that while these painted designs are typical of Harappan sites they have very little in common with the other local artistic works either in style or in subject. The stamp seals comprise the most voluminous body of Harappan artistic products, yet they show an accomplished technique and a sound artistic sense quite different from the painted designs. Moreover, there are on the seals a number of animals and symbols that certainly were familiar in everyday Harappan life, yet with but few exceptions they do not appear on the pottery. Only one humped ox is seen on the pottery, which is strange, particularly when we consider that this typically Indian animal is repeatedly portrayed on the ware of Kulli and Mehi in Baluchistan, to which Harappa is culturally related. Other animals seen on the seals are wholly missing— the rhinoceros, tiger, water buffalo, crocodile, and elephant. There are no mythical or multiple beasts such as the seals have, no swastikas, and no writing—an almost invariable feature of the seals. Snakes appear in both media, yet never does the hooded cobra of the seals appear on pottery.[11] Humans are found frequently on the seals,[12] but none has the one distinguishing feature seen in Fig. 142 and noted on so many of the western painted examples—the upraised hands. Nor do we see concentric circles as an all-over pottery design as it was used on Harappan bone,[13] or the three-lobed rosette used on the statuary and beads.[14] One point in common is the ordinary buffalo, often engraved on the

[11] M-d, pl. cxvi, 29.   [12] Ibid., pls. xii, 12-14, 17-19, 22; cxvi, 1, 29.
[13] Ibid., pl. cxxxii.   [14] Ibid., pls. xcviii; cxlvi, 40, 49, 53; clii, 17.

seals,[14] and the probable buffalo of Fig. 156. But how different they are in style. The painted version lacks any of the spark of life that animates the engraved examples. The only convincing points of similarity, in style as well as subject, between the painted pottery and other media rest in the peculiar form illustrated in Fig. 174 and in the plant designs, both of which we have already noted as characteristically local conceptions. We may also assume that the most common of all the forms of painted pottery animal life, the peafowl, was a local concept, though even it is not represented in any other medium. The jungle fowl, another local element in the painter's repertoire, is also not represented on the seals. With the plants we have the two seals representing pipal leaves[16] and the common painted equivalent seen in Fig. 121. Several seals show foliage or plant formation like that in Fig. 136,[17] and at least one has the form seen horizontally in Figs. 132-3.[18] A certain resemblance exists between the animals of Fig. 145 and the votive animal figurines in pottery, though the crudeness of the latter may mean that the likeness is fortuitous. But no resemblances in skill or style exist between the quite accomplished sculpture and the living forms depicted on vases.[19]

This surprising rarity of agreement in subject and style between phases of artistic expression, each characteristically Harappan, at first suggests that the painted pottery makers were racially distinct from the remainder of Harappan craftsmen. Yet this is unlikely in view of the likenesses just noted, few though they be. More important, the shapes and composition of the painted vases do not differ in any way from the far greater number of undecorated vessels. Consequently, we must believe not that the people who made them were different from those who worked on seals and statutes, but that the tradition by which their craft was governed was different. This tradition not only dictated the motifs in the geometrical patterns but the kinds of

14 *Ibid.*, pl. cx, 302-25.
17 *Ibid.*, pls. xii, 16, 20-1, 25-6; xiii, 17.
16 *Ibid.*, pls. xii, 18; cxii, 387.
18 *Ibid.*, pl. cxvi, 30.
19 With the possible exception of the human figures in Fig. 142. There is also a basic likeness in idea between the form of fig. 89 and the stepped crosses in shell inlay (*M-d*, pl. clv, 34-5), though the Amri example fig. 90 is much closer to the Harappan shell form.

animals that could be shown as well. Apparently only the style, not the subject matter, could be bent to the will of the artist; and only where the painter was not bound by well-established tradition, as in the plant designs, could he express himself in a natural way. The complete absence of so many of the tropical animals of the seals shows with certainty that the painted versions do not represent a true cross section of the common animals of the early Indus Valley but ones that through custom were permissible among painted pottery designs.

We have already had occasion to remark on the improbability of such a strong western tradition being the result of borrowing or casual contact. It must have been the result of direct inheritance from a people, or groups of people, who in earlier times are known to have used the same motifs and conventions west of the borders of Baluchistan and India. Thus one comes inevitably to the conclusion that among the racial stocks making up the Harappans was an element from the west sufficiently large to have emplanted, and to have ensured the survival of, their particular technique of pottery decoration. Side by side with these people was an even larger group who may be considered as native to the Indus Valley if one may judge them by their seals, sculpture, and certain restricted categories among the painted pottery. Finally, the indisputable likeness between the products of these two groups shows that by the time we find them, they had already amalgamated into the homogeneous stock which we have called Harappan.

The skeletal material from Mohenjo-daro and Harappa itself, not all of which is positively Harappan in period, shows an assortment of Proto-Australoid, Mediterranean, Alpine, and the Mongol branch of the Alpines as the anthropological types represented.[30] If any reliance can be put in these findings, it would seem that along the Indus was an extremely mixed population. Our study so far has not enabled us to identify any anthropological group from the remaining objects, nor is there any possibility of doing so with any degree of accuracy for so late

[30] M-d, p. 107. In M-d, 1927-31, p. 631, Mr. Guha has changed his opinion on the question of the Proto-Australoids, calling them, instead, "Caucasic."

[94]

a period in the history of man's development. It is quite possible that the Indus Valley had played host to such differing anthropological types even before the artistic traditions with which we have been dealing had become crystallized. Certainly by the beginning of the chalcolithic age intercommunication between groups displaying distinctive artistic styles was so common that we may presume even then a very considerable mixture of anthropological types throughout western Asia.

IV

Though it is not the purpose here to trace the origins of the Harappan peoples, we have seen that the evidence given by the painted pottery shows two broad cultural strains, one western in origin, the other Indian.[21] It is difficult to be specific about the source of the western element without drawing on conjecture, but certain generalizations may be made.

In the case of Iran proper, there are a host of sites yielding painted pottery. These, it will be noted, are confined mostly to the southern and western reaches of the country. All of these show numerous designs and conventions common also to Elam and Mesopotamia on the one hand and Baluchistan and Harappa on the other; yet neither is sufficiently close either in technique or design to demand the conclusion that Harappa is its direct descendant. Consequently, though a definite relationship between the two geographical groups cannot be denied, one can do no more than to postulate a cultural and racial bond of a type so mixed and so remote in inception that the means by which it came about is indiscernible. There are, however, certain important likenesses between Harappan designs and those of Sialk III. Because these likenesses are also shared with Halaf, they will be treated later, in the discussion of the relationships to that Mesopotamian site. With the later levels of Hisar, Giyan, and the

21 The term "Indian" must be used here with caution, for there is no certainty that this element in the Harappan make-up was autochthonous in India. At most we can only say that the "Indian" designs are those in which there are plants and animals recognizable today as Indian, as well as less distinctive objects and patterns done in the same style; but we have as yet no indication as to where in the East this strain in the Harappan make-up first emerged as a creative self-expressing force.

so-called Nehavand pottery, we are dealing with material which at this point is of secondary value, since it is later than the period during which the Harappan style crystallized.

With the Elamite sites, such as Susa I, Musyan, and Khazinah, we have much the same situation as that observed in Iran proper, though the larger number of correspondents with Harappa—particularly with Musyan and Khazinah—gives the impression of a closer bond between Elam and the Indus than was the case with highland Iran as a whole. Susa II, again, is too late to be considered as a source of Harappan designs.

Passing to Mesopotamia, we have with the ware of Jumdat Nasr much the same situation as with Susa II: a product coetaneous with Harappa, showing through certain likenesses of design and technique a relationship through common inheritance. One very striking likeness, shared in this period only by Jumdat Nasr and Harappa, is the bowl-like potlid.[22] So peculiar and restricted a form implies direct borrowing one from the other, though there is not sufficient evidence as yet to show which is the originator.[23]

It will be remembered that the products of al-'Ubaid have figured but little in our comparisons with Harappan ware. The preoccupation of the al-'Ubaid potters with elementary geometrical patterns, and the use of only the simplest curvilinear designs, has produced little common ground on which Harappa and al-'Ubaid might meet.[24] Nevertheless, the relationship of al-'Ubaid with the cultures of Elam and Iran is well accepted, and we

---

[22] *Jemdet Nasr*, pl. lxvii, 25-7; *M-d*, pl. lxxxii, 36-44.

[23] The relationship proposed by Dr. Frankfort between the barbotine vessels of Tell Asmar, near Baghdad, (*O.I.C.*, no. 16, pp. 47-53, figs. 32-3; no. 17, fig. 14) and those of Mohenjo-daro (*M-d*, pl. lxxviii, 16) is unconvincing, for they do not correspond in shape, size, or manufacture. Actually, the Asmar examples are remarkably similar in technique to those of early Nuzi, with which at that time Dr. Frankfort was not acquainted (*Nuzi*, pl. 42, P).

Another seemingly-Mesopotamian form in Harappa is the high-footed offering stand (*M-d*, pl. lxxix). But this need not represent direct borrowing by Harappa, since its presence at Samarra is ample evidence of an antiquity as great as the designs the two cultures held in common (*Samarra*, abb. 69). Hisar I in its high-footed bowls also approached this form.

[24] The al-'Ubaid patterns show a greater similarity to those of Amri than to any others of India or Baluchistan.

have already had occasion to point out the certain bond between the last two and Harappa.

The very early ware of Samarra has entered into our comparison with Harappa on numerous occasions, yet the likenesses noticed had to do with individual details rather than with designs as a whole or the spirit in which they were rendered. The basic similarity is not as close as that of the Elamitic wares, or even those of Persepolis and Hisar. Consequently, we can assume only an indirect relationship between the two, along with the certainty that they both stem from the same painted pottery tradition of Iran and Mesopotamia.

With the designs of the Halaf culture we come to a more delicate situation. We have already remarked on the impressive number of similarities between this distant school of design and Harappa. Certain of the likenesses are shared also with Samarra, Musyan and Susa, and Iran proper, and may only be considered as motifs held in common by peoples remotely and anciently related to each other culturally. Other designs are shared only by Harappa, Halaf, and Sialk III; and still others only by Harappa and Halaf. There is, in fact, a closer artistic bond between Harappa and Halaf than between Harappa and any other western group.

It would be well to consider for a moment the relation of Sialk III to Halaf. There can be no doubt that Sialk III is contemporary at least with the later phase of Halaf culture. The almost exact similarity between the peculiar rendering of tigers at the two sites, the preference for, and the detailed treatment of, grid patterns, as well as the rendering of other geometrical motifs, leaves little doubt of the close relationship between the two.[25] The question at once arises: Are the two the same in culture? That they are related, there can be no question. We have already noted in relation to an earlier period, Sialk II, the similar use of connected lozenges as a central decoration in both cultures, and there is a certain likeness of design between Sialk I and the

[25] Compare the following Sialk and Halaf designs: *Sialk*, pls. lxvi, S. 1813; lxxi, S. 38; lxxiv, S. 1691: lxxx, C, 14; lxxxiii, A. 8, B, 6; lxxviii, C, 11 and *Arpachiyah*, figs. 77, 1; 78, 3, 8, 37, 7, 27; 54, 4. Numerous Sialk-Samarra relationships also exist. See, for example, *Sialk*, pl. lxxii, S. 1765, and *Samarra*, abb. 16, nr. 16.

Proto-Halaf ware of Mersin.[36] But close examination reveals fundamental differences of design and technique that preclude the possibility of considering them—Halaf and Sialk III—as culturally identical. These differences are obvious and need not be dwelt upon here. Suffice it to say that we have at Sialk what appears to be an intermixture of inherited Halaf repeat patterns with typically Iranian conceptions of composition and of animal forms. Along with this we have such striking isolated Halaf designs that it is certain that the influence was not one of inheritance alone, but that frequent intercommunication, and exchange of ideas and products, existed between the two.

Returning to Harappa, another question arises: Did not this so-called Halaf influence on Harappa really originate in Sialk? Reasonable as this would seem from a geographical viewpoint, it is not supported by fact. It will be remembered that Sialk and Harappa did not share exclusively any decorative patterns. Many are common to the three—Halaf, Sialk, and Harappa—but a considerable number in addition appear only at Halaf and Harappa: notably, the intersecting- and continuous-circle patterns. This would indicate with some certainty that Halaf was the culture of origination, and that Sialk was only a stopping place in their progress eastward.[37] That it was more active than Sialk in disseminating its culture is further substantiated by the presence at Sialk of several of what may be called typical Halaf patterns and animals, and the striking absence of correspondingly typical Sialk conceptions of animal designs in Halaf sites. Nor should we disregard the Halaf characteristics noted by Mackay among the post-Harappan vessels of Jhukar culture at Chanhu-daro.[38] It

36 *Liv. Annals*, xxvi, pp. 51-73.

37 In the notable similarity between certain painted pottery patterns of Sialk II and the Shahi-tump burials we have another interesting pointer to show Sialk intercommunication with the southeast. There is between the two cultures an obvious discrepancy in period—one which should probably be explained as the survival, in an outlying quarter, of much earlier racial and cultural traditions—but at least it serves as a further indication of the rôle played by Sialk as a transmitter of cultural traditions from west to east. Since the Halaf-Sialk-Harappa relationship dates from the time of Sialk III, the Sialk-Shahi-tump contact—which stems from Sialk II—would be the forerunner of that eastern extension of Halaf-Sialk culture which in Sialk III was to reach the Indus.

38 *Ill. Lond. News*, Nov. 21, 1936, p. 908.

is exceedingly likely, then, that an appreciable number of people brought up in the artistic tradition of the Halaf culture went into the make-up of the mixed race which was to evolve as Harappa.[29]

Finally, we can say that no portion of the western tradition of pottery decoration discernible in Harappan ware can be interpreted as Semitic. Neither is it related to the burnished red ware of Uruk and Anatolia, nor to the burnished gray ware of northern Iran as seen at Tureng Tepe, Hisar II and III, and late Sialk.[30] With the various fabrics of Anau we have similarities only in the most elemental patterns, and from Afghanistan we have as yet no painted pottery in any way comparable to Harappa.

It will be seen, then, that the western element in Harappan designs cannot be equated exclusively with any one western culture, though the relationship to them collectively as a single cultural family is obvious. The likeness to Halaf in particular puts emphasis on that group as the principal contributor in the mélange of peoples and ideas that made up this element in Harappa as a whole. Actually, the impossibility of identifying the whole of the Harappan western element with one particular foreign group need not bother us, for it is neither essential to one's belief in the western influence on the Indus peoples, nor consistent with historical practices elsewhere, that all the immigrants to a favored land should come from one foreign group, or at one time. One can well believe that the Indus Valley throughout its history was repeatedly called upon to act as host to wanderers from the increasingly desiccated lands of Iran and Mesopotamia.

V

It was stated in the beginning of this study that the Harappan culture was non-Aryan. Everything that we know about the culture of the Indo-Aryan conquerors of India confirms this statement. And if we are correct in supposing the Harappans to have been in occupancy of the Indus Valley during the greater part of the third millenium before Christ, we can be equally

✓ [29] See also the similar conclusion reached by Mallowan in *Iraq*, III, pt. 1 (Spring, 1936), p. 42.
[30] "Rapport . . . de Tépé Sialk," *Syria*, XVI, pp. 229-46.

certain that no such host as the Indo-Aryan invaders appeared during that period. For such an invasion would have brought about inevitable and drastic changes of which there are no signs in the observable finds of Harappan sites. Nor should one believe that the Harappans could have withstood such an onslaught. Their peculiarly unwarlike nature would have made them easy prey to any determined intruding force. The Harappan cities, had their existence coincided with the Indo-Aryan influx, would have been the first big prizes to fall, for they were in the direct southward path of any invaders coming in over the Hindu Kush (Harappa itself is actually south and *east* of the Khyber Pass) and on the watercourses that afford a natural highway for incursion from that quarter. Moreover, though the early literary evidences of the Aryans in India are vague, all the indications point to a contact with a greatly inferior people, certainly not with a group as advanced as the Harappans or their successors of the Jhukar culture. Thus, though the evidence as a whole is negative, the Indus cultures give further support to the current view that the Indo-Aryans entered India at a period considerably later than 2000 B.C.[31]

[31] The close similarity to Harappan painted ware seen in the pottery of the Jhukar period, which followed Harappa, and its basic Indo-Baluchi character, suggests that the Indus Valley remained undisturbed by any markedly foreign invasion for some considerable time after 2000 B.C.

INDEX

INDEX

MAP

The location of each site mentioned in the text is shown on the following map. Each is there designated by a numeral as listed below. In so far as is possible, these run consecutively from left to right, and from top to bottom within related areas.

al-'Ubaid	14		Moghul-ghundai		32
Amri	67		Mohenjo-daro		55
Asau	35		Mustang		51
Arabjo Thānā	73		Mūsyān		16
Aspachiyah	5		Nāl		47
Astarābād	25		Nehāvand		19
Baghdad	11		Nineveh		6
Bampūr	39		Nuzi		8
Bandhni	64		Othmanjo Buthi		74
Bijnābād	34		Pandi Wahi		57
Chagar Bazār	3		Periano-ghundai		53
Chanhu-daro	77		Persepolis		30
Chauro	65		Pokhran		68
Cheshmeh 'Ali	22		Rām-rūd		37
Damb Buthi	63		Sakje Geuzi		1
Dāmin	41		Sāmarra		9
Deh-bid	29		Sampur		50
Dhāl	66		Sayyid Maurēz		49
Dhillanjo-kot	75		Shāhi-tump		50
Ghāzi Shāh	60		Shahin-kotiro		72
Giyan, see Tepe Giyan			Shahr-i-sōkhtah		36
Quandi	61		Shāh Tepe		23
Halāf, see Tell Halāf			Sialk, see Tepe Sialk		
Harappā	78		Sam		18
Hisār, see Tepe Hisār			Tal-i-pir		33
Ja'farābād	17		Tal-i-rēgi (Khanū)		32
Jhangar	62		Tal-i-Sang-i-sākh		30A
Jhokar	54		Tal-i-siāh (Mādavān)		31
Jundat Naw	12		Tal-i-akau		31
Kalāt-i-girl	38		Tando Rahim Khān		58
Kanchar	69		Teberan		21
Kishān	27		Tell Asmar		10
Kaukin	42		Tell Halāf		2
Khojus Landi	71		Tepe 'Aliābād		16
Khazinah	16		Tepe Gawra		7
Khutras Buthi	70		Tepe Giyan		20
Khūrāb	40		Tepe Hisār		26
Khyber Pass	79		Tepe Sialk		28
Kulli	45		Tharro		76
Lohri	59		Tureng Tepe		24
Lohunjo-daro	56		Ur		15
Mari	4		Uruk		13
Mehi	46		Zik		44

www.ingramcontent.com/pod-product-compliance
Lightning Source LLC
Chambersburg PA
CBHW030628270326
41927CB00007B/1348